Does He Speak Welsh?

by

John Scott

Red'n'Ritten Ltd.
Editor: Joan Stanley

Published by Red'n'Ritten Ltd,
17 Kings Barn Lane,
Steyning,
West Sussex
BN44 3YR
© Red'n'Ritten Ltd. 2008

ISBN 978 1904278 68 9

A CIP Catalogue record for this book is available from the British Library.

Printed by Marston Book Services Ltd.

Cover Artwork and Illustrations: Mike Avery

Editor: Joan Stanley

Does He Speak Welsh?

By

John Scott

"Ydy e'n siarad Cymraeg?"
Does he speak Welsh?

In this delightful, childhood memoir the author takes us back to the time when he was evacuated from wartime Newcastle, with his mother, to stay with an elderly aunt in Wales. It was a time when the local people all conversed fluently in their own native tongue, and the diverse characters he met, uncles, aunts, and cousins several times removed, were a fascination for the young lad. Not least, was his Uncle Bob the local baker who introduced him to the mysteries of bread-making, which stayed with him all his life.

A year or so later, mother and son left the safe, slow lifestyle of seaside Pwllheli, and its surrounding mountainous countryside, to rejoin his father in Newcastle and then onto York just in time to survive the German bombing raid on that city. The book follows the family's fortune and the author's returns to Wales in adulthood.

Although the author spent a relatively short time of his young life in Wales, his stay during WW2 and his subsequent visits have had a lasting and profound effect on him and his family. *Hiraeth* – that nostalgic longing for the distant mountains of Wales will ever be with him.

To Meriel,

for keeping my feet

firmly on the ground....

One

We were burying Father's ashes.

"Poor John," said Mother.

"Why poor me?" I asked.

"Because you are going to have to make this trip all over again for me, aren't you."

And she had been right.

Here I was again in that same graveyard with that same mountain looking down on me. I glared at it resentfully. It was more of an ambitious hill, a mere mound strewn with bracken and rock. But it had been a mountain when I had gleefully conquered it as a boy.

Was it laughing at me now? Daring me to have another try?

I declined the challenge. I stood over the family grave, and I was a small boy again on my first journey into this heart-tugging, infuriating land called Wales - long, long ago in the 1940's during the dark, early days of the war ...

I had seen pictures of evacuees in the newspapers and on the news-reels, leaving London for the country - in case their city got bombed. Crowded onto the railway platforms were hundreds of boys and girls with labels tied to their coat lapels. They were all carrying little suitcases and had their gas masks in cardboard boxes hanging from their shoulders. And their parents were hugging them and waving, 'Bye bye.' On the news-reels everyone looked happy and the announcer was positively cheerful, as if they were all going on holiday. I sat in a darkened cinema and felt uneasy about the whole business.

When, over the dinner table, the possibility of me becoming an evacuee came up I was appalled. Was I to be despatched weeping, labelled and clutching my little suitcase to some country wilderness?

Mother piled the dirty dishes into the sink. "I don't like the idea of leaving you here…"

"You'll have to go with the boy. I can't go," said Father.

"But will you be all right?"

"Of course I will…"

And so it was decided that Father should stay in Newcastle - to keep the railways running in his 'reserved occupation'. I was to be 'evacuated' to Mother's aunt in Wales, and Mother was to come with me. My relief was immediately tinged with guilt. Was not this running away? It was true that German planes were regularly flying over the Tyne, but no bombs had actually fallen.

So it came about - a sad goodbye to Dad late at night on a near deserted railway platform in Newcastle, with no cheerful crowds and no newsreel cameras. Two of us headed out into a forbidding, blacked-out world on a miserable journey that lasted all night; sitting in dimly lit railway carriages making frequent stops at darkly sinister stations, which appeared out of the darkness as ghostly, fleeting glimpses of life. Noses pressed against the window, we looked for the station names where we had to change. Then, cold and resigned, we lugged our suitcases down long empty platforms looking for the next connection, which was always, "Just over the bridge."

And we found it eventually - a silent row of empty, unlit, unheated coaches standing forlorn and engine-less. We climbed on board and sat in semi-darkness until we felt the gentle thump as the engine was connected, followed by clanking, a hissing of steam and voices. Then the lights came on in the carriage reassuring us that there really were people out there somewhere. Off again, the hooded lights of the station went past the window and finally disappeared leaving us gently rumbling and rattling through what seemed to be endless darkness.

At Caernarvon another connection was waiting for us - a miserable little locomotive that looked like a toy compared with the roaring, hissing, giant expresses that I knew in Newcastle. And instead of a vast waiting line of gleaming carriages, this engine was connected to a shabby goods van and just one coach.

Two men on the engine and the guard in the goods van watched unspeaking as we climbed into the coach. It seemed this train was running just for us. We chugged and puffed out of the station into still more darkness. If Wales and its promised mountains were out there, somewhere, I could not see them.

Gradually the darkness gave way to a grey light and we could make out barren fields, with dry stone walls. Dawn was breaking and we stopped at a place called Afon Wen.

The arrival did nothing to cheer me up. There were no buildings or houses, just two wooden platforms linked by a footbridge, standing at the edge of a listless, grey sea. The locomotive came to rest snorting steam as if it were offended at being forced to visit such a place. Afon Wen, according to Dad's meticulously hand written instructions, was our last connection.

We got out of our carriage and stood on the empty platform with our luggage. The guard, still unspeaking, unloaded two milk churns from the goods van and climbed back inside. He reappeared with a whistle between his lips and a flag under his arm. The whistle was blown, the flag held high and an arm waved back from the driver's cab. The engine hissed and sizzled back into life and set off backwards, the way it had come.

Mother and I were abandoned - left on the edge of a cold seashore in a world that appeared either asleep, or more worryingly, dead. As the noise of the train died away we were aware of another sound - the restless rustling and rattling of pebbles on the beach as dull, depressed looking waves heaved and fell listlessly. In the dawn light we could now see for miles; this made the feeling of isolation even worse.

The railway line along which we had come from Caernarvon was joined by another track running along the coast in both directions. In the far distance the morning mist covered shapes that could be mountains. We stood on the wooden platform with two milk churns for company feeling like the only people left in the world.

The written instructions were clear: 'Connecting train from Harlech will arrive at 6.40am.' So we sat on our cases and Mother opened the 'bait tin', which we had been slowly emptying of biscuits and sandwiches as the long night had progressed. There was just one scrambled egg sandwich left. But as I held it a soggy corner curled away in my fingers and snapped off, falling through the cracks in the timber planks and onto the pebbles below. A sudden, squawking scrabble of thrashing wings and beaks tore the pieces of egg and bread to pieces.

We had thought we were alone, but unknown to us the seagulls had been watching. I decided I did not like this place at all.

"When is the next train coming?"

"Soon."

"What if it doesn't come?"

"It will."

"But what if it doesn't ?"

I had a sudden fear of being left here - abandoned forever. But something was moving in the empty countryside; an old van was slowly making its way along a country road. We watched this sign of life with rising interest as it took a turning and came towards us down a narrow track. The van was parked; a man got out unloaded a luggage barrow from the back and strode onto the platform. It was the milkman come for the milk. He gave us a curt nod as he loaded the churns into his van and slammed the doors. Not a word was spoken. We watched in silence as even this small piece of life disappeared from sight along the coast road. Our world was empty again. I bit my lip and shivered. What were we doing here? Why had we come?

"There's the train," said Mother suddenly pointing to a puff of black smoke miles away on the horizon, where the distant sea merged into what I could now see were distant mountains. Slowly, agonisingly slowly, the train came along the coast towards us, stopping and starting until at last it reached us. Again it was just one engine, one coach and a goods van. The guard got out with his flag and walked up and down the platform looking very important and shouting "Afon Wen! Afon Wen!" But nobody got out, because there was no-one on board. We opened a carriage door and heaved our cases into a compartment.

"Last bit," said Mother cheerfully. "Soon be there now."
And she was right. A scattering of houses appeared, and a harbour; there were boats forlornly stranded on banks of dark, glistening mud. We entered a station and the train came to a stop, the engine snuffling and panting contentedly against a set of buffers. We had arrived at last at Pwllheli.

This was new to me - a railway line that had come to an end. In Newcastle the great mainline locomotives never ran out of track, they were always on their way to somewhere, either rushing up to Scotland or down to London. But here the railway line just ended in a little station and that, for me, was disturbing.

Where were we? How could there be no more railway lines? Had we really come to the end of the world?

The train might have arrived, but the station was still shut. There was no-one about, not even a ticket collector at the barrier, and it had started raining. Mother picked up the heavier of the two suitcases while I swung and lugged the other one along two-handed.

"It's not far to Aunt Nell's." Mum walked out of the station into the rain and I followed.

The street was deserted, not even a scurrying cat, and we were facing a row of shops with a rusty Victorian iron colonnade running along the front. The shops were shuttered and barred, and the colonnade had a glass roof with bits of grass sprouting from the guttering. Along the

We had arrived at last

upper storey of the building ran the words: Bon Marche. It all looked tired and forlorn and there was an unpleasant, pungent smell of coke. My eyes followed my nose and I found its source; snug up against the end of the department store was a huge, rusty gasometer. It was quite the most dismal exit from a railway station that I had ever seen and it got no better.

Turning a corner we found ourselves in a large square with puddles settled in the uneven ground, and some shabby, sheeted-down amusement stalls and a roundabout.

"There's a fun fair," Mother said, trying to cheer me up. I sniffed. It was nothing like the fun fairs on the town moor at Newcastle. There we had flying chairs, great soaring wheels, and motorbikes rattling and roaring around the Wall of Death. It was nothing like that at all.

A mean terrace of dirty grey pebble-dashed houses appeared with shiny-wet, black slate roofs, each house with an identical two square yards of garden fronted by a low pebble-dash wall. I could not believe that this was going to be my home.

"We're early," said Mother opening the gate of the last house in the terrace. "I wonder if she's up yet." We knocked on the door and waited. For the first time there was a hint of uncertainty in Mother's voice.

My Great Aunt Nell was certainly not up yet. We stood in the rain for fully ten minutes before the door was unlocked and I had my first sight of her - a small, plump, bleary-eyed figure in a candlewick dressing gown and furry slippers. She gaped at the pair of us standing wet and bedraggled on her doorstep, with our suitcases. Her first reaction was to clutch her dressing gown tightly across her chest. Then she gathered her senses and we were drowned in a torrent of Welsh.

I had arrived. But I was in a foreign land, and I did not know a word of the language.

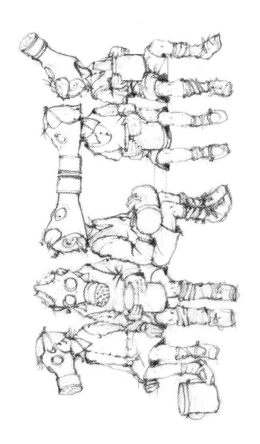

The air raid shelter

Two

I stared up at the ceiling of the little box room at the front of Aunt Nell's house, day-dreaming about Newcastle and why I was there ...

Every few days a German plane appeared over the city. The sirens sounded and we put our exercise books away in the desks, stood up as we had been drilled, and filed out of the class room and down to the air raid shelter, which had been dug at the edge of the school playing field.

"They're looking for ships in the Tyne. Reconnaissance raids. The bombers will be coming soon," I was told.

In the underground shelter, sitting in rows with our gasmask holders on our knees, we listened to the bangs of the anti-aircraft guns. My gasmask holder was a tin tube that had been dropped and kicked so many times the lid had become twisted. Sitting there in the dark tunnel of the shelter I nervously kept slackening the top – just in case. And then one morning in the shelter the lid would not come off and I got into a panic. I saw myself lying there as the gas came down, choking to death, the only casualty in Form IV. But an arm came over my shoulder and took the battered tin tube out of my sweaty hands. It was dropped back into my lap a few seconds later with the lid removed. I expected to be told off by Mr. Williams for not looking after it properly, but he never said a word.

The only good thing about sitting in the shelter, apart from missing lessons, was that sometimes we saw a German aeroplane. Mr. Williams stood at the bottom of the concrete steps where shafts of daylight came in. Sometimes he would beckon to the boy nearest to him and point upwards. Once when it was my turn I saw the German aircraft high in the sky followed by a line of black puffs of smoke from the bursting anti-aircraft shells.

"I can see him!" I said.

The whisper would run along the rows of boys sitting tightly, knee to knee, on the narrow slatted benches in the darkness.

"Scottie's seen a Jerry!"

"That's why I'm here," I told myself. "The bombers will come ..."

But I did not want to be here. I felt I had run away to another land where I did not understand a word they said.

Aunt Nell had been a teacher, and in my eyes she still looked like one. Her lips always seemed pinched in vague disapproval and she had a habit of rolling her eyes upwards while talking, as if in weary acceptance of the inadequacies of everybody around her.

I was told her father had been the minister at one of the chapels in the town – and, therefore, someone of great importance. She had married the curate who had eventually taken over from her father as leader of the chapel. But her husband had died young - leaving her a widow.

My aunt, I was told, was someone of authority and significance in the town; a judgement, which as a small boy I accepted, at the same time being slightly puzzled why someone so important lived in such a small house.

Later that day Mother took me for a walk around the town and I was relieved to see that the place was inhabited. Our walk was a very slow affair. Every few yards we were greeted by people kissing my mother and crying, "Helen bach!"

They then fell to chattering in that same foreign tongue that flowed over my head, until someone noticed me standing there. Suddenly they were all talking about me. Then came the phrase that I would come to hear so often that it became burned into my soul, "Ydy e'n siarad Cymraeg?" (Does he speak Welsh?)

"Nargy" Mother would say, and all eyes would look down on me.

"And how old are you, then?" one woman asked in English with a lilting, sing-song Welsh accent.

"Twelve."

"Twelve is it, that's nice."

"He's tall for his age, isn't he?"

"He's got your eyes, Helen."

An embarrassed silence followed until the Welsh started up again.

I tried to guess what they were saying by the way they looked at me. In the end I went into a dream until the conversation ended and we progressed a few more yards up the street until someone else shouted, "Helen bach!" and it started all over again.

It was just the same in the shops - ladies came round the counter to look at me, shaking their heads in amazement for some reason that I could not understand. Mother it seemed knew everyone.

When we did eventually get back 'home' to Auntie Nell's and we could talk in English I felt that someone had taken stoppers out of my ears.

"How do you know so many people?"

Mother was surprised at the question, but we did not have so many friends in Newcastle. "This was my home. I lived here until I was your age, and then we had to move to Northumberland."

"And you left all your friends here?"

"All of them."

"Weren't you lonely?"

"You just got on with it - like *we* have to just get on with it."

I bit my lip and said nothing.

Mother was watching me closely. "Your grandmother cried when we got to Newcastle station."

Cried? Adults did not cry. "She didn't! Why?"

"Because the railway porters were shouting at each other in that Geordie accent of theirs and she couldn't understand a word. Your grandma said, 'Oh Helen bach, we've come to a foreign land.'"

"Newcastle, foreign!" I laughed.

"It was foreign to us!" said Mother. "We spoke Welsh. We only learned English at school, like you learn French. It was our second language." Her tone changed. "So you see all this moving about ... it happens a lot," she said briskly. "And it all works out for the best in the end."

I felt a twinge of sympathy for my long dead grandma, but she could speak English. I certainly could not speak Welsh.

Three

As soon as I went through the front door of Aunt Nell's house I collided with the bottom of the stairs. The two living rooms were so full of furniture I had to squeeze round them to find somewhere to sit.

I established myself in a corner of the front room where Mother had found me a small card table on which I piled the few games and toys I had brought with me and my half-completed balsa wood Spitfire. This was my little world. I pinned a big map of France on the wall with the Maginot and Seigfried Lines marked on it, so I could follow the war on the radio. There did not seem to be any war, but there was a heated discussion about me sticking pins in Auntie Nell's wallpaper. Even though it was in Welsh I could tell what was going on, and as no order came to take down the map it stayed where it was.

At Auntie Nell's I learned to like 'stunch': bits of potatoes, vegetables, cheese... in fact any edible bits left lying around were crushed into a hot pan and fried almost black on both sides. Eaten with a dollop of brown sauce it was not at all bad – until I suddenly crunched into a re-heated, soggy Brussels sprout, lurking like a depth charge in the fathoms – it was revolting.

Every night, no matter what the weather, Aunt Nell went out leaving Mother and I alone either to play cards or Ludo, or to listen to the radio. I never knew where Aunt Nell went, but she always got back before I went to bed.

Then one night there was an even longer conversation than usual in Welsh, which obviously concerned me. Mother was not pleased and Aunt Nell rolled her eyes further upwards than usual; she even shrugged her shoulders so I knew it must be something serious.

What had I done now?

I soon discovered my transgression. I had been swinging on the clothes line in the tiny back garden. That had produced a letter from Aunt Nell's landlord who obviously lived within spying distance: the clothes line had been fastened to a drain pipe and he had feared for his guttering.

Obviously the new young tenant was being closely watched and that made me nervous.

Mother took a deep breath. "Get your hat and coat on, we're going to your Aunt Katie's for the evening."

I had never heard of Auntie Katie, so this walk to see her in the black-out was something of an adventure, a break with the stifling routine of listening to the radio or other mundane activities that passed the winter evenings.

Out we three went into the blacked out streets, the beams of our torches picking out the kerbs and potholes, past the shuttered shops in the main street, until we came at last to a row of terrace houses with their doors opening straight out onto the pavement. In the darkness I saw an extra wide, front window, partially obscured by net curtains. Behind the glass were two worn, wooden shelves suspended on cords hanging from hooks in the ceiling. And on the shelves looking lost and lonely were two loaves of bread.

Aunt Nell pushed open the front door and a bell on a spring rang furiously above our heads. She called out something in Welsh and a voice answered from inside. Mother and I followed Aunt down a narrow passage. There was a door-less opening on our right leading into the tiniest of rooms lit by the dimmest of gas mantles. Half the room was taken up with a battered wooden counter, and on the walls behind it were rows of shelves. There was an overpowering smell of freshly baked bread mingling with the smell of boiled fish.

The door at the end of the dim passage was opened and we walked into the slightly brighter glow of Auntie Katie's parlour. The whole scene was lit by another dim gas light. It was a tiny room overpowered by a black-leaded oven and fire range, which almost filled the length of one wall. A wooden table and two chairs were jammed up against another wall and an old leather sofa was backed up against a Welsh dresser filled with an Aladdin's cave of little ornaments, trinkets and photographs. The rest of the furniture consisted of one shabby armchair softened by a rug that looked like a dog blanket.

The smell of fish now overpowered that of bread. It came from what looked like little more than a passage leading off the parlour. It was in fact the kitchen – a white-washed, lean-to extension at the back of the house. I could see a pan simmering on an iron gas stove, a stone sink with a wooden draining board, and two crude pipes thrusting out of the wall and ending in large brass taps.

The frail, grey-haired figure in black standing over the stove was my Auntie Katie. I was introduced in Welsh. She looked at me for a long time, chewing her bottom lip, and then she patted the top of my head and stroked my cheek. I thought for a moment that she was going to cry. Why was everyone around here so miserable?

Mother and Aunt Nell sat side by side on the sofa in front of the fire. The only other comfortable chair was the one with the dog blanket. That clearly belonged to someone so I perched myself on one of the chairs by the table. In front of me was set a knife and fork, a plate of bread and butter and a tea pot lurking under a badly stained, knitted, woollen tea cosy. Aunt Nell saw me perched there and said something in Welch.

"That's Uncle Bob's place," Mother explained.

For goodness sake! Why couldn't Aunt Nell talk to me directly in English?

I moved to the chair at the other end of the table as Mother and Aunt Nell started talking with Aunt Katie who was joining in the conversation from the kitchen.

I was trapped. The room was hot, tiny and claustrophobic and the overpowering smell of boiled fish made me feel sick.

Great Uncle Bob

The bell on the front door jangled and Aunt Katie emerged from the kitchen wiping her hands on a cloth. The bread shop apparently was open all hours and I had to get out of my chair to let her pass. I could hear the murmuring voices in the shop before she returned to the kitchen. The ritual was repeated several times, with my aunt drifting like an uncomplaining wraith between kitchen and shop. And all the time the talk flowed between the three women and I sat in silence understanding not a word.

The bell jangled yet again, but this time violently and the front door was banged shut. There was the sound of bolts being put into place and heavy footsteps in the passage. I leapt up. If someone or something came through that door at speed they would send me and my chair flying. The door did open and I came face to face with a big man with piercing eyes and big, black, bushy eyebrows. I was aware of a creased, crumpled, black jacket curiously speckled with white powder and worn over an equally scruffy waistcoat, which was minus a number of buttons. Across the waistcoat was draped a large gold watch chain. His white shirt was collar-less, and had a shiny brass stud hanging from the top button hole. It looked as if it lived there permanently without ever having been introduced to a collar.

The man's mouth dropped open in surprise at the sight of me, and the spiky hedge of eyebrows shot up in astonishment. An exclamation escaped his lips, which made Aunt Nell, on the sofa, bristle indignantly. Mother was on her feet in an instant, speaking quickly, and I realised that my presence was being explained in some detail. This I gathered was my Great Uncle Bob.

He took off his jacket, hung it over the back of the chair, staring at me all the while. Aunt Katie was now in the room, too, silently holding a steaming plate with a huge piece of boiled fish on it and a pile of mashed potatoes. Bob nodded at her curtly and she put the plate on the table. Mother meanwhile had finished explaining. Great Uncle Bob eyed me and I eyed him.

"John, is it?" he said at last and thrust out a gorilla-like paw.

My hand disappeared inside his and I was surprised how soft it felt.

"Yes," I said.

He grunted and picked up his knife and fork and started to eat. The women who had been silent throughout all this resumed their chattering, but in more subdued tones. Occasionally Uncle Bob would noisily clear his throat for silence and address my mother or his sister, but he never spoke to Aunt Nell. Sometimes he would remove a large fish bone from his mouth with his fingers and point it at them to give greater emphasis to his remarks. I was fascinated with what he did with those fish bones. Having used them as pointers in his discussions he would then use them as tooth picks. And having carefully excavated what was stuck between his stained, horse-like teeth, he would lick the bones carefully and lay them in a row around the edge of his plate like trophies from a hunt.

Aunt Katie took away the empty plate, with its neat row of bones, and silently put a bowl of rice pudding in front of him. That, too, disappeared in great spoonfuls. Uncle Bob dusted himself down with his napkin and regarded me across the kitchen table. There was a curious expression on his face. His mouth twitched. "John," he said in English. "Tell your Aunt Nell that they've got some batteries in at Jones's. She'll need them for her flashlight."

I gaped at him. We were all sitting within a few feet of each other. He nodded his head vigorously to confirm what he had said and then he gave a quick sideways nod towards Aunt Nell in case I had forgotten where she was. I swallowed hard.

"Aunt Nell, Uncle Bob says they have got some batteries for your flashlight at Jones's."

On the sofa Aunt Nell's ample chest was heaving dangerously.

"Tell your Uncle Bob," she said very slowly and deliberately. "Tell him that I have got plenty of batteries for my flashlight, thank you very much."

18

I looked back at Uncle Bob and he was looking at me, with what I now realised was a half suppressed grin on his face. He turned one ear towards me, cupping his hand around it and clearly wanting me to repeat the message.

"Uncle Bob," I said nervously. "Aunt Nell says …"

Mother sprang to my defence. She unleashed a torrent of Welsh over Uncle Bob's head. The tenor of it was clear enough, though I did not understand a word and I was aghast. Surely this terrible, giant of a man would rise up in fury and destroy us all, but instead he stared at the table and said nothing. Aunt Nell joined in the tirade while Aunt Katie fled into the kitchen. I sat there petrified as the storm raged.

Great Uncle Bob had found a spare fish bone left on the table cloth and was doing some more excavating between his teeth. With no further contribution from him the row petered out. Auntie Katie reappeared from the kitchen like a little mouse creeping out of a hole, and the three women started talking to each other again, but in even more subdued tones.

After a few minutes I became aware that across the kitchen table eyes were watching me from under those bushy eyebrows. My Great Uncle Bob winked.

Why did my Great Uncle Bob not speak directly to my Great Aunt Nell? That little episode with the torch batteries was not unique. All their conversations were conducted through a third party: "Tell Nell this …" or "Tell Bob that …" Mother had only objected when I was drawn into the pantomime. One night, on the way home from the bread shop I asked Mother why.

"Oh dear," she said wearily.

Uncle Bob, she explained, had become the head of the family of four sisters and himself after both their parents died young. He had also become, in more ways than one, the bread-winner when he had taken over the family bakery.

Three of the sisters - one of them my grandmother - got married, but Katie did not. Instead she looked after the shop and kept house for Bob. But then Katie met a young sailor and wanted to get married, too.

"Aunt Katie wanted to get married!" I said incredulously, wondering how any young sailor could be interested in such a timid, grey, old lady.

"Your Auntie Katie was a very pretty girl when she was young," said Mother severely. "And that's the tragedy of it. Bob flew into a rage and forbade it. Terrible rows. Aunt Nell sided with Katie and persuaded her to walk out of the shop and live with her until the marriage could be arranged."

"But Auntie Katie isn't married."

"No she isn't - more's the pity," said Mother and she fell silent.

"So what happened?"

"Bob went storming round to Nell's and took Katie back, that's what happened?"

"Took her back …?"

"Took her back, yes. He stood there shouting and railing like some mad, old prophet in the Bible. And Katie went back with him, meek as a lamb. Just followed him back like someone bought in a slave market. And she's been there ever since - and that's nearly fifty years ago."

We walked on in silence while I had a terrifying mental image of Uncle Bob in a towering rage.

"Katie wanted to have children," said Mother. "She dearly wanted a little boy. So you see …" She hesitated and then went on quickly: "But instead she's spent the rest of her life looking after him, cooking, cleaning, trapped in that shop. That's what happened to your Auntie Katie."

Mother was upset. "So Bob and Nell have never spoken to each other directly ever since. Nell goes round to see Katie every night without fail just to make sure she's all right. And that's been going on for nearly half a century."

"And Auntie Katie's still there in the shop."

"Isn't she just!" Mother muttered something to herself in Welsh. "John pet," she said softly, "some people can be very selfish, and very cruel and very unkind. Don't you ever be like that."

I felt very wary of my Uncle Bob.

After that visits to Auntie Katie's became part of my life. Often Mother and I would leave the gloom of that dim, gas-lit back parlour early, making the excuse that I had homework to do. But the real reason was fish and chips. Aunt Nell thought fish and chips were common, so we never dared tell her where we were going, and there was always the fear that some friend of Aunt Nell would see us.

Mother and I would lurk in the darkness until we saw the shop was empty, and then we would push aside the black-out curtain and go in for two penny packets of chips with plenty of vinegar.

After the gas-lit gloom of Auntie Katie's parlour the warmth, brightness and the smells of that fish and chip shop took us into another world; it lifted the spirits. But once outside again we had to eat our chips furtively in the darkness of a shop doorway like a couple of conspirators on Guy Fawkes Night. Somehow it made them taste even better. Then we would go for a walk to get the tell-tale smell of chips and vinegar off our clothes before going back home to Auntie Nell's.

Four

School in Wales was not the nightmare I had feared. With Father having to move all over the country with his job on the railways I already had half a dozen schools under my belt. By now I accepted the ritual of being the 'new boy' with weary resignation. I had learned to my cost that not all schools progressed at the same speed. For instance, I missed the lessons where you learned to link up individual letters into proper 'joined-up writing.' As a result I evolved my own unique, often illegible system. And the first time I saw A + B = 6 written on a blackboard I thought everyone had gone mad. I had missed the beginning of Algebra, too.

I thought it was my lot in life to start dazed and confused at the bottom of every class, struggle until I got somewhere near the top, only to move on to another town and another school. And now here we were again, only this time in Welsh. But this little school was different. The teachers were friendly. I was the son of 'Mrs. Scott, Miss Whitchurch -that-was' and to them that appeared to be important.

On my first day I sat at a desk in an empty assembly hall and a lady teacher gave me some exam papers. "Just answer as many of the questions as you can." So I did, they were easy.

An hour later she was back. "Well done," she said glancing through them. "You're quite a clever little lad, aren't you?"

No-one had ever said that to me before. Suddenly the son of 'Mrs. Scott, Miss-Roberts-that-was' felt a little bit special. The teacher nodded her head in approval. "We'll try and teach you a bit of Welsh, too. Then you'll know what everyone is going on about, OK?"

"OK."

Everyone in the playground was, of course, talking Welsh. I joined in a game of football with a worn out tennis ball. I was a bit bigger than most of the boys and I scored easily between the two school cap goal posts. "You speak Welsh?" one of them asked.

"No."

"Good shot that was."

"Thank you."

The boys went back into their gang. The girls were more sedate and stood around the playground in groups chatting, rarely breaking into a game of tig. One or two of them, I noticed, watched me from a distance; the new English boy was a curiosity.

In the classroom the Welsh of the playground gave way to English. It came fluently from the teachers and hesitantly from the pupils. I was impressed and a little jealous. They already knew two languages. The girl at the next desk to me had long black hair almost down to her waist and dark eyes to match. And she was pretty. "Where you from?" she whispered.

"Newcastle."

"Where's that?"

"Way up north."

She relayed this information in Welsh to her neighbours who all stared at me anew.

At school I was enjoying myself. I was taught the Welsh alphabet and intrigued to find that 'w' was a vowel pronounced 'oo' and that 'dd' was pronounced 'th.' Even more strange was the discovery that 'll' was a slightly rude noise, like the hissing of an angry cat. Added to this came the information that the language was strictly phonetic; if you knew the alphabet, which I soon did, you could read it aloud quite easily, even if you did not understand a word you were saying.

After school sometimes I found myself walking part of the way home in a group and some of them, usually the girls, would try to teach me Welsh, demanding to know the Welsh for 'good morning,' 'good bye,' and 'thank you' and shrieking with laughter when I got it wrong.

I came to dread weekends, because 'going to chapel' had gradually become an issue. For Aunt Nell chapel was the high-spot of her life, religious and social. She took ages getting dressed on a Sunday morning - applying lipstick and powder, which appalled me. Why did a woman of her age put on lipstick? She was old! But every Sunday there was an atmosphere in the house - a tension in the air. I was developing an instinct, which told me when I was under discussion and I soon realised that Aunt thought that I, too, should go to chapel. Mother said she could not see the point when I would not understand a word. I did wonder if Mother did not want to go to chapel herself and if I were being used as an excuse. We did not go to church in Newcastle. But the constant eye rolling and pursed lips eventually won. Sunday morning saw me in my suit, my tie neatly tied and my shoes polished.

Stepping out of the house, I was immediately aware that the atmosphere of the town had changed. People emerged out of hiding in their best clothes and while they were very polite to each other in the street I noticed the critical eyes that were being cast over each other's Sunday apparel.

We joined the stream of people in their Sunday-best. So I went unwillingly to chapel, but when I got there I was fascinated. It was like no other church I had ever seen. It was huge for one thing, with a narrow gallery high up around the walls. And it was packed. But the real surprise came with the first hymn. The noise was overwhelming. Everyone sang as if they wanted to send the rafters, the beams, and the whole roof flying off to heaven. While the women's voices went soaring gloriously upwards there would come a surging, growling roar from the men. No one seemed to be singing the same tune, but somehow it all fitted in together. And in the front pew, turned around and facing us, was an ugly, cross-eyed, fat, little man flailing his arms and conducting the whole congregation.

With my new knowledge of the Welsh alphabet I found I could follow the words in the hymn book. After mouthing them to myself for

25

The Minister up in his pulpit

a few verses I, too, started to sing. Mother and Aunt Nell eyed me with some amusement. The trouble was I did not know who to sing with - the women or the men. Whoever I tried to follow the tune soon shot out of reach, either going too high or too low, I lapsed into silence letting the sound wash over me.

But when the fervour and excitement of the singing ended the boredom began. The minister up in his pulpit did not wear a vicar's collar, nor did he read out what I would call 'proper prayers'. He seemed to be making them up as he went along. And when he came to his sermon the lilt of his voice nearly sent me to sleep, until, that is, he suddenly got excited and began shaking his fists in the air. I thought he was having a fit as his voice rose to a high, rhythmic, singing shout. The congregation kept joining in and shouting, "Alleluia!"

At the end of the service everyone spilled out into the street, all still strangely excited and elated. They gathered on the pavement chattering to each other, Mother and Aunt Nell included. I had enjoyed the singing. I just wished I could have understood what they were all so excited about.

Five

Father came to visit us for a week during the Easter holidays. Hurrah, we could go places and we could talk in English. He had brought maps and compasses, and timetables for the railways and buses. And there was a present – a toy anti-aircraft gun: gunpowder caps fired rubber pellets. I peppered Auntie Nell's ceiling bringing down imaginary Stuka dive bombers.

"Right," said Dad, "which mountain are we going to climb?"

"The big one we can see from the town." I had already marked a challenging hump on my distant horizon.

Maps were spread over the table and Father was soon tracing routes with his forefinger. "Yup, we can walk up that one. Map says it's called Yr Eifl. There's a proper path. Now how do we get there?"

Out came the timetables. The long columns of figures were complicated, but we found a bus that would get us close to the hill in the early morning. Getting back home again was the problem: on its return the bus only went to Caernarvon.

"Trains," said Dad, and out came another timetable. Yes, there was a train back to town from Caernarvon changing yet again at Afon Wen.

Throughout all these discussions I was aware, out of the corner of my eye, of the disapproving figure of Aunt Nell.

Early next morning, with our knapsacks stuffed with sandwiches, flasks of tea and extra sweaters, we stood waiting in the square - the open space where the fair had been left trapped and abandoned. It had arrived for an intended three day stay and found itself marooned and without petrol when war was declared. I had discovered that defiantly on Saturday afternoons a few stalls would open and music would blast out from the loudspeakers. They only had two records: 'Run Rabbit

29

Run' and 'We're Going To Hang Out The Washing On The Siegfried Line.' But there was no cheery music this morning.

In fact we were so early the whole town appeared to be asleep; no sign of life and no bus. Eventually we heard the whine and crunch of gears long before we saw our transport rasping and coughing its way around a street corner into the square. It was old and shabby, with a matching driver in a crumpled uniform and a battered peaked cap. He opened the bus door and looked at us, but we were not invited inside. Instead he groped under his seat for a huge leather money bag, which he balanced on his knee. "Where do you want to go, then?"

Father struggled with the Welsh name. "It's the stop before the village of Llithfaen," he said.

There was a puzzled look on the driver's face, firstly at Father's pronunciation and secondly, it seemed, that anyone should want to go there. We paid our fare and the tickets were handed over, then the driver got out and carefully shut and locked the bus door behind him. Adjusting his cap, he walked off to the public toilets in the corner of the square.

We stood there clutching our tickets beside a locked and empty bus, and with Father trying hard not to laugh. "He's absconding with our money," he whispered, but the driver did return smoking a thin, hand-rolled cigarette.

Two men appeared from around the corner and joined us in a neat queue beside the bus stop sign.

"Bora da," said the newcomers.

"Bora da," said Dad brightly. The two men looked at each other.

"English are you?"

In two words the foreigners had been spotted.

" 'Fraid so."

"Ah," and that ended the conversation.

The driver with his cigarette dangling from his bottom lip unlocked the bus door, and with a nod of the head motioned us to go aboard. He remained outside slowly smoking his cigarette in deep, long, appreciative drags. Pulling a fob watch on a chain from his waistcoat pocket, he looked at it carefully for some time; clearly he did not believe what he saw; he wandered off across the square.

"Going home for breakfast now," Dad whispered and I started to giggle.

But the driver had only gone to check his watch's accuracy against the chapel clock.

He took the cigarette from his mouth carefully blowing and pinching out the burning fragments between finger and thumb. The unburned paper and tobacco he rolled back into shape and slid into his waistcoat pocket. Back in the bus he settled himself in his seat and made a great show of examining his watch yet again. The key was turned in the ignition, the engine woke up, reluctantly, and we were away, grinding slowly and noisily through the gear changes.

Dad winked at me. "Luxury Express Pullman service here we come."

The first village we reached was called Y Ffor, and was little more than a tiny row of houses on either side of the road. It did not have a bus stop, but the bus stopped anyway. The driver got out and disappeared into what appeared to be the one and only shop. Through the window we could see him buying potatoes, some carrots and a lettuce, all the while chatting unhurriedly with the proprietor. Back he came not only with his own purchases in a small sack, but a box of someone else's groceries as well; these he pushed under the front seat.

At the next village our two other passengers got off, but not before they had had a lengthy chat and shared a few jokes with the driver. Now we had the bus to ourselves and our mountain was getting closer, and looking steeper by the minute.

First, there was another village called Llanaelhaearn and this one showed signs of life; there were people. Our driver was constantly pipping his horn and waving to passers-by until suddenly he slammed on his brakes, and he was out of the vehicle in a flash. The engine was left running while, cap on the back of his head and hand on hip, our driver was locked in deep conversation with an elderly man on the pavement. Cars squeezed past us giving friendly toots and the two men replied with friendly thumbs-up signs. Time ticked by and Father looked at his watch and shook his head in disbelief. The driver returned, to stand on the step, half in and half out of the bus, still chattering.

At last, we were off again. We turned away from the main road onto a narrow, twisting country lane with the mountain, our mountain, rising up ahead of us. Then a postman appeared cycling towards us, a lonely figure in this bleak expanse of countryside. Where had he come from? Where was he going? Perhaps the driver was worried about the same questions for we stopped and there was an unhurried chat through the bus window. It appeared to be a regular mail call; the postman handed over two letters, which our driver balanced carefully against the inside of the windscreen while he in turn handed the postman three other letters from his ticket bag.

While all this was going on I took advantage of the delay to study 'our mountain' more closely. It was not a dramatic rocky crag topped with snow, but its sides were steep enough to make me feel a little alarmed. Half way up the grass and bracken gave way to large banks of broken rocks. This was not going to be easy.

The mail call was coming to an end. There were cheery exchanges and waves and we were off again, only to stop after a few minutes in the middle of nowhere; just empty countryside all around, a mountain looming above us and no sign of habitation anywhere.

The driver turned and looked at us. "If this is the place you want this is it," he said cryptically. Outside there was a rusty bus stop sign leaning drunkenly against a partially collapsed dry stone wall. I looked through the window at fields and a landscape devoid of as much as a munching sheep. Even Father was taken aback by the barrenness.

"You'll be back here again at ten past three, won't you?" Dad asked. "That's what the timetable says …"

"Does it? Yes, I suppose it's about then. Depends on special deliveries, see."

I remembered the box of groceries under the seat.

"But you'll definitely be here?" Dad insisted.

"Never missed yet," the driver winked at me. "What you doing getting off here, then? There's no-one at the farm down there these days. Derelict it is, but no-one's bothered to take this bus stop off the time-table, see."

"We're going to climb that," I said proudly nodding towards the mountain. The driver looked at us both and chuckled.

"Well that's nice. Can't see the point of climbing things like that, myself. You've only got to come down again, haven't you? Can't stay up there for ever. Seems a waste of time to me, but there you are …"

He thrust the long gear lever noisily into place. "Don't get lost! See you about three o'clock this afternoon, then. Otherwise it'll be tomorrow - same time."

There was a grin on his face. The bus left us and as it disappeared I had the same feeling that I had when the train left Afon Wen. All around us was that same empty stillness - small fields pock-marked with outcrops of rocks and patches of bracken, girdled by dry-stone walls.

There was a gate tied up with rope on the opposite side of the road and a faint track leading across a field, before it disappeared into a fold in the land. 'Penlan Farm' said a crudely painted notice lying in the field.

Father laid his map on the top of the wall and showed me where we were. He always liked this bit. I think it made him feel like a general briefing his troops. We had got off the bus at this stop, because Father thought he had seen on the map a quick route up the mountain.

There had always been doubts in our family about Father's map reading and his obsession with short cuts.

Once while crossing Ilkley Moor on a week-end ramble he could see no reason why the path we were following on the map went round in a great loop. He led Mother and me on a short cut and we squelched straight into a bog. This time there was no bog, but having climbed through a gap in the dry stone wall we faced steeply rising ground. And it got steeper. As we climbed higher we were faced with loose banks of broken stone that would have defied an Alpine goat.

Father brooded over his map and without saying a word started walking along the side of the mountain in what I could see was the opposite direction to the summit. We were heading towards the village, which was the bus's next stop and which was the proper starting point for the path to the summit. I had absorbed this much from the map, but I said nothing.

Eventually we did pick up the path. Father treated this as an achievement so we rewarded ourselves with our first drink. Already the countryside was stretching out below us and there was a faint line of blue sea on the horizon.

"Right, here we go!" said Dad starting purposefully back along the way we had come, this time on the path. At first it was comfortably broad and the land sloped away gently on both sides, but as we got higher the slopes grew steeper. Sometimes the path was cut into the side of the mountain and I found myself nervously resting one hand against the rock as I walked.

"You OK?" Father kept saying. "You OK?"

No, I wasn't OK. I was frightened. We came to a narrow ridge along which the path ran to a small plateau. This was the summit. I was no longer frightened - I was terrified. I made the last few yards walking behind Father with my eyes staring at my feet and with both hands gripping his trouser belt. At the very top was a concrete post set in the middle of a stone platform - a map triangulation point. I put my arms around the post and hugged it until I stopped shaking. The ground all around us fell away to nothing. I thought I was on the top of the world and at any moment I was going to fall off.

Dad un-slung his haversack and sat with his back to the post, pulling me down beside him.

"Now that was something. Yes?"

"Yes."

He patted me on the knee. We were looking down on the approaches to the Menai Straits and what seemed to be toy ships tracing white lines in the water. And to the south far across the fields was another sea and the faint trace of smoke from a train running along the coast. My sense of terror slowly subsided. We ate our sandwiches in silence.

"Something you have to do before we go down," said Dad. "Put your hands on top of that post to steady yourself and then jump up."

"What for?"

"I'll tell you what for when we get down again. Just do it. "

So I did as I was told, my hands clutching the concrete, just in case. After that we came down the mountain very slowly and carefully. When we reached the village I looked back and could not believe it.

Father looked back, too, and then at me nodding his head in approval. "Something for us both to remember, eh?" he said softly "Something we did together."

He went into a sort of reverie and spoke no more until we found the bus stop in the village. Then he said abruptly, "I don't really like mountains."

"Why not?" I protested.

"You wouldn't understand."

"I would!" I said indignantly.

Dad looked sad. "They're so damn permanent, that's why. That great chunk of rock will still be there after we're all dead and gone."

It was an odd and puzzling thing for him to say. He saw me looking at him curiously and immediately perked up.

"Anyway," he said brightly, "every time you come past here when you're older you can look up at this mountain and you can shake your fist at it, and say, 'I've beaten you. I've climbed you with my Dad, so there!' And you'll remember this - always."

"Right," I said and I shook my fist at the mountain. "I've climbed you, so there!"

But Father had something to explain. "Up on the top," I asked. "Why did I have to jump up and down?"

"Well now," said Dad. "If someone says that they've climbed that mountain as well you can tell them, 'Actually, I've been higher than that one.' And you have, too – about six inches higher when you jumped." It was Dad's idea of a joke.

As we waited for the bus Father had another thought. "Don't tell your Auntie Nell or your Mother about that last scary bit will you, or they'll never let us out again."

"Promise," I agreed.

The bus driver was surprised to see us waiting in the village and not at Penlan Farm. "Should charge you for an extra stop, but I'll let you off."

"We got right to the top," I told him.

"That's nice."

I got the impression that he thought we were harmless idiots.

Our mountain receded into the distance, but the shape of it stayed against the horizon and in my mind.

The bus driver was in a hurry and there were no stops to chat on the way back.

"Late for dinner," whispered Dad.

We caught the train back from Caernarvon weary yet triumphant. The mountaineers returned.

Six

That week with Father passed all too quickly. We watched as the cormorants in the harbour dived for fish and then perched on rocks with their wings spread out to dry. We found a billiard hall hidden away behind some shops and I learned to play snooker. Father bustled around the table whistling happily to himself.

"No whistling!" came a shout. The ugly, little, cross-eyed man who conducted the singing in the chapel was in charge of the billiard hall. Father pulled a face at me and I tried not to laugh out loud. But I was annoyed. How dare that man shout at my Dad. Anyway, how could a cross-eyed man play snooker? Dad played his next shot with his eyes crossed and I had to smother my giggles. The man from the chapel glared at us.

With Father's return to Newcastle my world again closed in around me. Mother had gone sad and quiet, but she did her best to compensate for Father's absence by taking me on walks.

On one walk along the sand dunes she pointed out a little island off the coast with a small white lighthouse. "That's St Tudwals - your granddad worked on that light. While he was there he met and married your grandmother who lived here in Pwllheli. After that the family moved to the Coquet Island off Amble in Northumberland."

"It must have been fun living on an island," I said.

Mother shook her head vigorously. "Not when the weather was bad and the food ran out. And we had a German Zeppelin paying us a visit when we were on the island light off Northumberland. That wasn't much fun."

"You never mentioned Zeppelins," I protested. "Tell me about the Zeppelins."

"I'll save that for when there's nothing on the wireless," she teased.

Saturdays were not quite as bad as Sundays, when the prospect of chapel loomed, but here in Wales there was no prospect of a football match or sailing a boat in the park, as there had been at home. So I took to wandering, trying to find somewhere new to explore.

One Saturday in the main street I bumped into three boys from my class with whom I played football in the school yard.

"Where're you going Scottie," they asked.

"Nowhere. Just walking."

There was a quick conference in Welsh.

"We're going up the Garn. Want to come?"

This came from William, clearly the leader of the trio, the other two members being his little brother Dai and their friend Robert.

"Up the Garn? What's that?" I said.

"It's a mountain ..."

As there were no mountains nearby that I could see I thought they were having me on.

"Won't you need ropes and things to get up a mountain?" I asked suspiciously.

Robert and William laughed, but little Dai clearly did not understand what I had said; the others explained to him in Welsh and he grinned.

"Not that sort of mountain," said William.

I was not convinced.

"All right then, where is it?"

"Just up the road – come on."

Disbelievingly I followed them along the main street. We turned into a side road lined with little terrace houses with their front doors opening onto the pavement, each house had a lovingly polished black slate doorstep and the walls were covered with that ubiquitous grim, grey pebble dash. But I noticed with growing interest that the road was going up hill. The houses came to an end, and suddenly we were out in the country and, yes, there it was – a mountain. It was really a hill made up mainly of grass and bracken and a few rocks, and it nestled so close to the town that when you were amongst the houses you could not see it. But now, as if to assert its presence, I could see it was crowned by what looked like a small concrete pyramid.

Little Dai pointed, "That's the Garn."

William pushed open an iron sheep-gate and we walked along an overgrown bush-shrouded lane. A five-barred gate provided a gap through which I could see a path leading across a field to the summit. The boys were over the gate in a flash and I joined them. In that field there was an immediate sense of freedom, no fences, no roads, no barriers only an open mountainside invitingly waiting. Half a dozen sheep stopped cropping the grass and stared at us with silly haughty expressions on their faces. 'What are you doing here?' they appeared to be saying. William and Robert ran towards them flapping their arms and they scattered half-heartedly, but stopped as soon as the boys stopped, turning indignantly to stare once more at the intruders.

William and Robert had left the path and were going along the side of the Garn.

"I'll take you up the proper way," said Dai. By now the other two had disappeared and there was just Dai and me walking sedately up the gently ascending path. I wondered where the other two had gone, but before I could ask, "This Newcastle," said Dai abruptly. "Big place is it?"

"Really big," I said proudly.

"Bigger than Caernarvon?"

I had only fleetingly seen Caernarvon, but replied confidently enough, "Much, much bigger. They build ships there – ocean liners, huge ones."

Little Dai was clearly impressed, and still curious. "So what have you come here for?"

That was a sensitive question. I hesitated. "My Mam thought we'd be safer here for a bit."

I was surprised how easily the Welsh expression 'Mam' had slipped out instead of my more usual 'Mum.' Was I already adapting to my environment? I suspected that even my Geordie English was developing a Welsh lilt.

"Great view," I said changing the subject, and it was. We were surrounded by soft swathes of tufted grass broken by patches of bracken. As we climbed I could see a Welsh world laid out at my feet. The town lay snugly below us: the harbour, the houses, and the railway line that had brought me; I could pick it out meandering its way along the coast until it faded into a grey distance where more mountains, real ones, lurked on the horizon.

Dai and I reached the top and I took a deep breath and did a slow, full circle search of the horizon; it was a chequered green and brown landscape of stone-edged fields, with sheep sprinkled about like gently moving confetti. I identified the mountain that Dad and I had climbed and pointed it out to Dai. My eyes swept on picking out Aunt Katie's house, then Aunt Nell's. And then I saw something else nestling close to the side of hill: a still, silent place, with a high stone wall around it and an ornate wrought iron gate. Inside were row upon row of gravestones. My eyes hovered over it momentarily. But on the Garn's summit I discovered something of much more interest - the concrete pyramid had a brass ring set into the top proclaiming: Ordnance Survey Point.

"You can sit on that," said Dai, and I was being given the honour of being the first upon the summit.

Perched up there swinging my legs I heard voices. There was only one part of the summit where the land appeared to fall away steeply and it was from there that the voices came. William and Robert had circled the Garn and were climbing the steepest bit, an outcrop of rocks, just below the summit. I jumped off the concrete pyramid, not wanting to deprive the real mountaineers of their triumph.

William scrambled onto the tiny plateau, complaining, "You did it the easy way." He, too, climbed onto the pyramid, but instead of sitting on it as I had done he stood on it. He flung his arms wide, beat his chest with his fists and did a Tarzan yell. Robert and Dai cheered and applauded and I tactfully joined in. We all sat and had a rest, and I realised that little Dai was talking about me to the others…

"Big ships were they?" said William in English. .

"Yes, the ones that sail to America with all the famous people on board," I replied. They were silent.

"I think I'd better be getting back," I said. "My Mam (there was that word again) thinks I've just gone shopping."

There was another discussion in Welsh, which William translated.

"We'll take you down the other way, and then you'll know both ways up and down next time, OK?"

"OK," I said. And down across the fields we went, through another sheep-gate and abruptly we were back into a world of roads, and boundaries, fences and high stone walls. And through the iron gates of one wall at the side of the road I saw the silent rows of crosses that I had seen from the summit. My eyes lingered, but I hurried past after the others.

William produced a tennis ball from his pocket and we played football down the road passing it backwards and forwards - always with the risk of the ball careering down hill out of control.

There were frantic shouts from William, including one helpfully in English: "Catch it!" His precious tennis ball was disappearing rapidly down the hill and heading for the main street. We raced after it and as we neared the road we all crashed into a burly figure coming round the corner. He was carrying a huge basket, which went flying, Dai and Robert ended up on the floor and only William and I managed to keep our feet.

The figure we had run into remained upright, immobile as a rock, but from it came a roaring, angry torrent of Welsh. We had crashed into my Uncle Bob. He stopped in mid flow, recognising one of this young gang of ruffians. "What you doing with this lot?" he asked me accusingly, in English.

"They're my friends. They took me up the Garn. I'm sorry. We didn't mean to bump into you."

There was a pause, and his manner softened visibly. "You! Get my basket," Uncle Bob ordered and William did so very promptly indeed.

Uncle Bob then hauled young Dai to his feet. "You all right?"

"Yes Mr Ellis," said Dai, very respectfully.

Uncle Bob wagged his finger at all of us.

"If that basket had been full of bread you lot would have been for the high jump. Right! Your parents would have had to pay for it. Right! Right!" He glared at William as our obvious leader.

"Right," said William humbly.

"And don't play football in the street."

"No, Mr Ellis," the trio muttered.

"And your damned ball is over there under that car."

"Thank you Mr Ellis."

And with his basket up on his shoulder again Uncle Bob strode back in the direction of the bake-house.

William looked at me after he had gone. "How do you know Mr Ellis?" The gang exchanged glances, but it was I who was puzzled.

"He's my uncle, or really he's my great uncle. How do you know my Uncle Bob?" I asked.

It was Dai who answered: "Everyone knows Mr Ellis the baker, everyone."

Seven

Nothing moved on my map of the Western Front. I sat at my table in the tiny front room and cut out the balsa-wood framework for my Spitfire. The shapes were stamped onto thin sheets of wood and needed a special one-sided razorblade, with a stiff top edge to cut them out properly. My one and only blade was blunt, making it almost impossible to cut everything out neatly, and razorblades were in short supply. Mother found some two-edged ones, viciously sharp and difficult to handle. I insisted on using them and promptly sliced my finger, which started dripping blood all over Auntie Nell's table cloth.

"Should have newspaper down," she sniffed as Mother bound up my wound. Wary of razor blades from then on I never did get that Spitfire finished.

It was during one of those interminable evenings in the parlour at Auntie Katie's that Uncle Bob finished his dinner, put down his knife and fork and growled at me, "Want to see the bake-house?"

The women looked at one another in surprise.

"Yes please." Anything that broke the boredom of sitting deaf and dumb in that claustrophobic little room was welcome. Uncle Bob retrieved his black jacket off the back of the chair and took his torn trilby hat off the peg behind the door.

"Come on. Let 'em get on with their gossiping."

A new and wonderful world was about to open up for me – a world of huge ovens, hot baking tins and the overwhelming, intoxicating, never to be forgotten smell of freshly baked bread. I had no idea where the bakery was; as far as I was concerned bread just appeared in Aunt Katie's shop as if by magic. We walked a few yards up the main street in the blacked-out darkness and Uncle Bob turned abruptly into an arched passage way. It was only a door-width wide and had been cut through the line of terrace houses. We emerged between two garden walls, did a sharp turn right and arrived at a stable door set in a stone barn roughly plastered and white-washed. Uncle Bob produced a key, opened the stable door and switched on a light. He waved me impatiently inside muttering, "Black-out, black-out!" and slammed the door shut.

The inside of the barn was filled with huge, stout-legged wooden tables with well-worn tops, and beneath them were wooden shelves full of bread tins; still more tins were on the rickety wall shelves. And taking up the whole of the far end of the barn was a massive, shiny, black and chrome oven with two double iron doors standing one above the other.

Two more tables stood end on up to the oven doors, but these were swept clean, empty and waiting. Above them, resting between iron hoops in the ceiling, were half a dozen long poles with ends shaped like paddles. Under the one bare electric light bulb everything was eerily silent; you could feel the heat pulsing behind the oven doors.

Uncle Bob had put on a white apron. He grasped a sack of flour around the middle and walked with it clasped against his chest, propping it on top of a huge metal bowl set on a square stand.

"Knife!" he ordered, pointing at one of the shelves. I found a knife handle, but no blade, just a slot where the blade should have been.

"Yes, yes," he said impatiently, "that's it." He shook the handle and a worn bit of steel barely an inch long appeared out of the slot. A quick cut and flour was pouring into the bowl, blowing a cloud of white dust back into his face.

"Learning Welsh are you?" he asked.

"Yes. Aunt Nell says I should …"

"Oh, Aunt Nell was it!"

I watched as water and some other ingredients went into the flour. Rising from the stand, which supported the bowl, was an iron contraption and hinged onto it a metal arm and prong. Uncle Bob pulled the arm down into the flour.

"Make yourself useful - switch it on."

He pointed at a switch on the wall, covered in fine white powder. When I pressed it there was a click and a whirring sound, and the bowl started to rotate. The metal arm swooped forwards and back stirring the contents. Uncle Bob leaned against one of the tables and eyed me while dusting his hands on his apron. "Want to learn Welsh, do you?"

"Suppose so," I conceded.

"Want to impress your Aunt Nell, don't you?"

"Suppose so …"

"Well now." He stood there with flour dusting the whiskers on his face, thinking. "See if you can say this …" I had to repeat it slowly several times before he was satisfied.

"What's it mean?"

"Never you mind what it means. You say that to your Aunt Nell. She'll be very impressed at you speaking Welsh. And tell her it was your Uncle Bob that taught you."

"Right, I will," I said, muttering the words to myself so I would not forget.

"And you've been going up mountains?"

I told him all about my two adventures and he listened carefully while keeping an eye on the revolving bowl. I was beginning to like my Uncle Bob. He was big, like a bear, and he growled a lot, but there was something mischievous about those eyes under those bushy eyebrows. They made you think he was going to laugh not bite. And yet Mother had said …

The flour in the bowl had congealed into a large, sticky mass. Uncle Bob kept throwing handfuls of flour along the inside of the bowl as the arm heaved the dough up and down.

"Do you make all the bread yourself?" I asked not a little overawed.

I was treated to some family history. Before the war his nephews - two brothers - had helped him in the bake-house and the three of them had supplied the whole peninsular with their daily bread. But they were called up and were now serving in the Merchant Navy, and Uncle Bob had to do the bread himself, alone, with Auntie Katie looking after the shop.

The bakery door opened and Mother came in. "Time to be going home. Have you been helping?"

I nodded.

Uncle Bob always treated Mother with great respect and the two of them were soon deep in conversation. I knew instantly that they were talking about me. Eventually Mother said, "Uncle Bob is wondering if you would like to help him in the bake-house during the holidays."

"Yes please."

And so I became an apprentice baker.

Eight

Had Mother and I not needed some groceries we would not have gone out in such a storm. We struggled against the wind and the rain, as we fought our way past the harbour. Huge, heaving, green waves bigger than I had ever seen were rolling in between the breakwaters. They swelled and surged around the harbour basin, making the moored boats dance and tug frantically at their ropes. I had seen the harbour at low tide, muddy and lifeless but that day it was angry and dangerously alive.

"That reminds me of Christmas," said Mother, turning her back to the wind so she could speak.

"What?" I shouted.

"Christmas," she yelled. "One Christmas we had on the island. It was just like this."

"You never told me."

"Let's get back home and I will."

And buffeted by the wind, we made our way home with the shopping.

In the kitchen Aunt Nell tut tutted about our wet clothes, and at mother's request she put the kettle on and made tea to warm us up, muttering that it would spoil our dinner.

"It was just seeing the waves coming into the harbour like that that reminded me," said Mother. "Imagine trying to take a boat out in that sort of sea."

"Impossible," I said, "You'd drown."

"Yes, but we did," said Mother.

I pulled a face. "That's silly. You should have waited until it was calmer."

"We couldn't wait – it was Christmas." Mother laughed at my bewildered expression. "I'd better tell you the tale from the beginning.

47

"We were living on Coquet Island, off Northumberland, and I was working on shore in Amble. As I said, it was Christmas and my brother Tom came up from London. He'd been working down there for some years by then. We were both going to go over to the island, but then this storm blew up.

"When we reached the harbour and I looked out to sea my heart nearly stopped.

"'I'll go and see the Harbour Master,' Tom said.

"So I waited on a concrete bench looking at the harbour mouth and trying to imagine a boat or even a ship trying to ride in on one of those waves.

"When he came back, he said, 'They say nothing is coming in or going out of the harbour today, and that's for sure.' I was sick with disappointment. Obviously I wanted to spend Christmas with my mother and father. We'd bought Christmas presents and everything. All we could do was take our suitcases back to where I stayed in the town.

"But I had had an idea. I told Tom to wait in the entrance hall of my lodgings while I went up to my room and got a large torch. 'I'm going to talk to Dad,' I told my brother. 'He'll know what to do. Come on.'

"So we walked along the front and then along the beach to where it was a bit more sheltered, though the wind was still whipping up the sand and stinging our faces. I sat on my suitcase and rested the big torch on my knees, and pointed it at the lighthouse. The island is not that far offshore and I started talking in Morse Code with the flashlight, and after a bit your granddad answered from the island."

"Wow!" I said.

"He signalled back and said that he would come and pick us up off the beach."

Wow, I thought again but I did not want to interrupt.

"There was an old converted lifeboat on the island," continued Mother. "We used it all the time, when we wanted to come ashore, but never in that sort of weather. I'll never forget it. Suddenly, there was your granddad in the boat, quite unconcerned, all snug in his big, woolly, navy blue sweater, smoking his pipe, and with one arm resting along the tiller. Close inshore the sea was not too bad, but further out I could see the waves, and the white horses going crazy."

Mother sipped her tea and watched Aunt Nell tidying up the kitchen.

"Go on," I pleaded.

"Dad turned the boat around and backed it towards us, but we had to wade out to reach him. I remember Tom took off his shoes and hung them round his neck. Very fussy man your Uncle Tom, didn't want to ruin his new London shoes, he said. Anyway we waded out with our suitcases on our heads and threw them in the boat – then we had to get in ourselves.

"'One each side,' shouted your granddad. 'And sharp about it!'

"I put both arms over the side of the boat and it promptly heaved up on a wave and lifted my feet off the sand. Tom was looking very pained, hanging onto the other side with his precious shoes still round his neck. I knew far more about boats than my city dwelling brother.

"'Do what I do,' I said, bobbing up and down in the water before suddenly swinging a leg over the gunnel. He did the same and we both ended up like drowned rats in the bottom of the boat.

"'Tuck yourselves under the seats,' said Dad. 'There's a bit of puff out there today.'

"A bit of puff! We sat on the bottom of the boat and pushed our legs underneath one of the cross bench seats. Dad accelerated the engine and a surge of water ran along the bottom of the boat and shot right up my skirt. I didn't really care any more. I was already soaking wet and freezing. As we moved away from the beach and got further out I could see the waves boiling themselves into an absolute fury.

"Dad took the pipe from his mouth and shouted, 'Hold tight! Going to be a bit lively like.' We were heading straight into those horrible, swelling waves, some of them white crested. The propeller came out of the water and roared as we were pitched up and down, and the prow of the boat kept slapping the water and throwing spray in our faces. That went on for several minutes until there was another shout from Dad: 'Hold tight!'

"I was holding tight! I saw that having headed straight into the force of wind and sea we were now attempting to turn and ride along with the wind behind us. But for a terrifying few seconds we were broadside onto the waves, wallowing dangerously in a trough before the propeller drove us forward again. Our lighthouse seemed to be bobbing about, appearing and disappearing above the waves. I'd done that journey dozens of times, but never in conditions like that and I wondered how we could possibly land on the island. But your granddad knew what he was doing. He steered the boat towards the sheltered side where the sea was a bit calmer, and I could see the tiny docking quay. Even there the sea was still heaving up and down as our boat came alongside and squealed against the old tyres hanging down the side. One of the light keepers was waiting for us in his oil skins.

"'Throw the cases ashore,' I told Tom and we did so as the boat rose level with the top of the quay. I had often stepped ashore from a rocking boat, but never when it was that rough. But I balanced with one foot on the gunnels, and as the boat came up I jumped and the keeper caught me.

"What about Uncle Tom?"

"He got ashore, too, and his precious shoes, and then he started complaining that his new suitcase had got scratched. Typical! Any way your granddad ordered us to get up to the house and get dry - as if we needed to be told."

Mother stopped and shook her head reliving every moment of it all over again in her mind.

"You won't remember the Coquet," she said. "You were only four when we took you on a visit, but there was a rough concrete ramp leading up from the quay to the lighthouse buildings. The concrete had been laid over broken rock and sharp edges were poking through; you could see the shovel marks where the wet concrete had been patted flat around them.

"Your grandmother was standing in the doorway, looking very worried and very cross, particularly when she saw we were soaking wet. She shouted into the house and Mrs. Jones, one of the other keeper's wives, came out and, I remember, she threw up her hands at the sight of us.

"Tom was whisked off to the bathroom in Mrs Jones's house and mother bustled me upstairs to ours. It had a big, cast iron bath in the middle of the stone floor. Usually it was cold and draughty in there, but it felt fine that day. I wallowed in lovely hot water, though I could hear angry voices downstairs. When I appeared in the kitchen, in my dressing gown, the voices came to an abrupt stop. Mother was at the sink and Father was in his armchair by the fire smoking his pipe, but looking very uncomfortable.

"'Helen bach, are you all right?' asked Mam. 'Stupid, stupid it was to bring you across in that weather. Stupid!' She glared at Dad. 'You have some tea and get yourself warm.'

"I'll always remember that kitchen with its stone flags and huge double oven and fire grate, all black-leaded and gleaming. The fire was always burning and there was always a kettle suspended over it, bubbling away, instantly ready for the next cup of tea. It was all so warm and cosy. Everything happened in there - it was living room, dining room and office combined: plates, mugs and cups up on the shelves, cupboards full of books and a huge pine topped table that was used as an office desk and for eating.

"Your granddad got up, knocked the tobacco out of his pipe, and left, muttering, 'Things to do ....' Your grandma just glared at him. She hadn't forgiven him for nearly drowning his family, you see. But I understood. Granddad wanted all his family together for Christmas, no matter what."

At the mention of Christmas I seized on an important matter that was missing from the story. "The Christmas presents! Were they all right, did they get wet?"

Mother laughed. "We dried them out, but your Uncle Tom made a fuss about his shoes. He'd dropped them into the bottom of the boat, of course, and they got all salt stained. What a fuss! But we still had a really good family Christmas on our island – a real good party and a good old sing-song."

Having at last got Mother into full flow about her life on her island I did not want her to stop even though Aunt Nell was making it very clear that she had heard all the stories before and wanted to get on with dinner. Never mind Aunt Nell, I thought, I wanted to know more.

"But what was it like living there?"

"Seagulls bring it all back," said Mother "That's what I remember, sea gulls crying - seagulls, and being lonely. When I was very young there were no children on the island except Tom and I, but he was older and got an apprenticeship ashore, so then I was even more lonely. I passed the time reading and playing the piano."

She was silent again – musing. Then I could tell she was making a determined attempt to be cheerful.

"We didn't just have parties at Christmas, you know. Any excuse really - birthdays, anniversaries… The women would get together to make the sandwiches, always the same they were - cheese, meat-paste, jam and homemade cake… And the parties were always in our front parlour, because it was the biggest room on the island, and it had a piano in one corner and a circle of arm chairs and sofas. The whole island would crowd in there – all eight of us. Everyone took a plate into the kitchen, filled it with sandwiches and cake, and sat in the parlour gossiping as if they hadn't seen each other for months."

"Your grandmother was in charge of the sing-songs. She'd sit down at the piano, and strike a loud chord, rattling the notes dramatically to increase the effect. Teacups would be raised and a little cheer would go up. Then she'd start to play something and everyone sang. You would have recognized some of the hymns. It was like a miniature version of chapel, everyone harmonizing. And then someone would sing by themselves, or recite a poem, just something to entertain."

"I bet you were good at it."

Mother smiled: "Well I could sing a bit in those days."

"But what about school?"

"I still had to go to school. Went off by boat on Monday morning; stayed in digs in the town during the week and came back on Friday night. The same thing when I started work. I used to joke that Billy was my best friend on the island …"

"But you said …"

"Let me finish - Billy was a goat and a very stroppy one, too. Given half a chance and he would sneak up behind you and butt you. Every day he did a round of the island with his two girl friends following him around in single file. He was their lord and master, you see, but the nanny goats were useful, for they kept us supplied with milk. We had gardens walled off to shelter the crops from the wind.

"There was always a wind moaning across that island, hit you in the face as soon as you went beyond the wall; but we grew good vegetables and that really saved us… One winter, when it was too rough for the supply ship to get in, the stores ran out and we lived off turnips for a week. I've hated them ever since. What I loved most about the food was the corned beef, cut thick, with baked potatoes. Cooked in the hot ash under the fire until the skins were hard and crunchy, you just brushed off the ash, split them open, put a dab of butter on each half and a dollop of HP sauce on top of that, lovely they were."

In the kitchen, Aunt Nell was becoming even more impatient, so Mother started setting the table, still talking in a lowered voice.

"My room had this one tiny window in a very thick wall," she said. "All I could see through it was a stretch of grass and beyond that sea, nothing but sea. It was like being in a prison really - a prison with sea instead of walls, but a very friendly prison. I would go out and collect the eggs for breakfast, and the other keeper's wives would wave at me from their kitchen windows. I would open the lid on the nesting boxes and push the hens to one side. There was always a lot of squawking and sometimes I got pecked. But it was wonderful, how warm those eggs were."

"But how big was this island?" I asked.

"Tiny," said mother. "Frighteningly so sometimes. The houses were perched on the only piece of high ground, and that was not very high. The whole island was just one field of spongy grass full of screaming birds and a few outcrops of rocks. I often thought that one big wave could sweep us all away and only the lighthouse would be left like a sand castle on the beach. Apart from the birds there were rabbits everywhere and some of them ended up in the pot, stewing with the vegetables from the garden."

I shuddered for I was a complete townie and was revolted at the idea of eating a rabbit. Mother paused, carefully studying the table to see if anything was missing. Then she became serious. "Your granddad got into trouble, because of that boat trip and not just from your grandmother."

"Why?"

"My landlady saw us go off along the beach, and as far as she was concerned we had just vanished. She didn't know where we had gone. People went out searching for us and it was only when the police telegraphed the island to tell Dad we were missing that they discovered we were all safe over there."

"Whoops!" I said.

"Whoops indeed!" said mother.

Nine

Dinner was served at last and Aunt Nell got a chance to talk about what she wanted to talk about – in Welsh, of course. In bed that night my thoughts were filled with lighthouses. I had no memories of visiting the Coquet as a child, but I had vivid memories of visiting Granddad's other lighthouses when I was older. The first one had been the most frightening.

"You got a good head for heights?" the impressive figure in Trinity House uniform asked me.

"Sort of."

"Come on, then!"

Once inside the tower I was immediately assailed by the smell of paraffin and metal polish. All lighthouses, I discovered, smelled that way. The concrete floor of the tower was painted a startling red, whilst the cast iron staircase that spiraled up the whitewashed tower was a shiny black; every sound we made echoed as if we were in a drum.

Granddad took a long handled device off a hook on the wall and explained: "Got to wind her up first." It was a huge key, which he slotted over a spindle protruding from a glass fronted box full of brass, cog-wheeled machinery; he started to wind. A chain went from the box to the very top of the tower and down again, and it had a lead weight fastened to the end. As the handle turned the weight rose. I was amazed - part of this great lighthouse worked on clockwork.

"Now up you go," Granddad said cheerfully. "Don't worry. I'm right behind you. Something soft for you to fall on."

Our footsteps on the metal stairs echoed loudly up the tower. We passed little windows, each with a small oil lamp and two matches laid beside it. As we climbed the tower was narrowing and we reached a small platform, only large enough for two people.

"Let me by," Granddad said. "And don't you move."

He edged past me and I immediately missed his comforting presence behind me; there was now no-one soft to fall on at all. I had a mental image of tumbling down the spiral staircase, like Humpty Dumpy on a bumpy helter-skelter ride, until I hit the blood-red floor at the bottom. Perhaps that was why it was blood-red, just in case …

Directly in front of us was a vertical ladder made of slabs of black slate set one on top of the other and only a few inches apart. Brass hand rails on either side also went straight up.

Granddad opened a metal trap door above our heads and light streamed in.

"You first," came the order as he pulled me around him. I hauled myself up on the hand rails, putting each foot between the rungs of the slate ladder. I was in the lantern top looking at glittering panels of glass prisms and the biggest electric light bulb I had ever seen. Granddad climbed up after me and dropped the trap door shut. "Watch this."

The panels of glass that focused and directed the lighthouse beam were set in a circle around the light. "Weighs tons they do," Granddad said. "Floating on mercury they are."

He pushed against one of the panels and the whole circular wall of glass prisms slowly revolved.

"Want to go outside?"

He opened a panel in the metal wall, which made up the lower half of the lantern top, ducked through it and went outside. I tentatively followed, and I found myself on the terrifyingly, light-weight, metal platform that ringed the top of the tower - a platform that had only two very thin safety rails. Granddad was leaning forward with his elbows on the top-rail, the wind tugging at his clothes and ruffling the wisps of hair poking out from under his cap.

"Have a walk round," he shouted. "Great views."

I edged my way round holding tightly to the rail. It was like being up in a balloon, but this was a land light, so I was not just looking out to sea, but down on houses in the little town. I could not remember where it was, Whitby perhaps, or Lowestoft? Granddad had served at so many of them.

"You OK?" he asked when I slowly reappeared from around the tower.

"Fine."

"Go down now?"

"Yes please."

The next morning, after Mother's story telling session, I realised there was something very important that she had forgotten to tell me about her island. "Zeppelins!" I said. "You didn't tell me about the Zeppelins."

She sighed, "I've talked enough about all that."

"No you haven't. What about the Zeppelins!"

"They were German airships."

"I know what Zeppelins are," I said indignantly. "I saw the Graf Zeppelin fly over Newcastle before the war. It was huge!"

"This one wasn't that big," said Mother. "The Germans used them for bombing raids in the First World War, and this one must have got lost. We think it stopped over the Coquet to try and find out where it was."

The idea of a lost German airship hovering over a lighthouse and trying to get its bearings was, I thought, hilarious. "You're joking!"

"I am not. We heard them up in the sky talking German."

"No!"

"Yes we did. They'd switched their engines off and they were just floating there – not very high up. In those days airships sometimes lowered people down in a basket to see where they were."

I was amazed. I lived in a modern age of Spitfires, Hurricanes and screaming Stuka dive-bombers, not Germans in baskets coming out of the clouds on the end of a rope looking for signposts.

"But what happened?"

"Nothing really. After a bit they started up their engines again and off they went. We were all quite relieved."

I came to the conclusion that my mother had had a very exciting life and I wondered if I would be lucky enough to have such adventures.

It was Sunday and we were going to visit yet another aunt. I thought this might be marginally better than going to Chapel and being sung and shouted at in Welsh. The once-a-day Sunday bus dropped us off just out of town in a shallow valley where a private road sloped up the hill-side. It led to the crest of the hill and a row of large expensive looking houses, each with a big front garden.

I was even more impressed when we went inside the one belonging to Auntie Liz. Compared to Aunt Nell's house and Katie's tiny back parlour this was a palace. The floor was polished wood and smelled of lavender, the rooms were huge and filled with expensive furniture; everywhere there were vases filled with flowers.

Tea was set out for us on a table in the dining room. Aunt Liz was small, quick and lively, doing all the talking while her husband William sat large, slow and quiet. While Mother and Aunt chatted my new uncle eyed me thoughtfully between sandwiches. Suddenly he said, "You can see Snowdon from the back garden."

That was nice, I thought, wondering what to say in response.

"Want to see it?"

Most of the sandwiches had gone so I nodded. Indeed the view from the back garden was wonderful. We were looking down at the sea, far to the west was a horizon of dark, pointed shapes.

"It's that one."

There were too many confusing bumps and ridges. In the end Uncle

William drew a diagram in the back of his diary, meticulously reproducing the distant sky-line. It seemed very important to him that I was looking at the right mountain.

"That one," he said at last. We both stared at it, neither saying a word for a long time and I wondered what next? OK, I have seen Snowdon - it's that big hump over there.

As the silence continued I thought it might be my turn to say something. "My Dad and I have climbed a mountain."

This, too, was greeted with a long thoughtful pause until, suddenly, "You can walk up Snowdon, you know."

"Can you?" But there was no more information.

We did a silent circuit of the garden looking at all the flowers while back in the house Mother and Aunt Liz were still talking happily.

A grandfather's clock in the hall whirred and clanked before striking three. Mother got up, "We must go. The bus will be here soon."

That provoked a one-sided discussion in Welsh between Aunt and Uncle: Aunt Liz talked quietly and firmly while Uncle William nodded his grey head slowly in acceptance. Out he went and through the window I saw him opening the door of the detached garage. Inside, I could see a car covered with white dust sheets and an extra blanket over the engine.

Uncle William removed the coverings and folded them neatly into squares revealing a highly polished, grey, Rover car, with a dazzling chrome radiator. I marvelled at this vision of wealth as Uncle slowly drove it out of the garage. Aunt Liz, meanwhile, had been upstairs; she reappeared wearing a smart black coat and gloves. The front door of the house was carefully locked, the rear doors of the car were opened and Mother and Aunt sank into the soft upholstery of the back seats. I could not believe it when Aunt motioned for me to sit in the front. I, too, was wrapped in the luxurious feel and smell of soft leather. Beneath my feet was a rich carpet, and arrayed in front of me was an intriguing row of glittering, silver-rimmed dials in a polished wood dashboard.

"Don't touch anything, John bach," whispered my Aunt Liz, as if I would have dared. Uncle William was about to get into the driving seat when his wife spoke to him quite sharply.

"Ah!" he said and went back into the house. He returned with an armful of shoe boxes, which he put in the boot. From his pocket he took out something heavy wrapped in a yellow duster. This he carefully unwrapped as he made his way to the front of the car. It was a silver cherub, which he slowly twisted into a fitting on the top of the radiator. After giving it a little polish with his duster Uncle William got into the car and pushed the starter button.

I felt very important driving back into town, and when we got to our street I could see all the net curtains twitching in the front rooms. Mother hissed at me, "Thank your Uncle William for the ride. It was very, very good of him to get his car out for us."

I did so with genuine sincerity, and as we waved them goodbye I asked, "Are they very, very, very rich?"

"He is a very important businessman in the town," said Mother.

"What were those shoe boxes for?"

"Never you mind."

Aunt Nell was trying hard not to be impressed, but her lips were well and truly pursed.

"Got the car out for you, did he? That'll give it a shock. Wasting petrol that is."

It reached down to the floor

Ten

Uncle Bob pulled a white apron out of a drawer and put it over my head. It reached down to the floor. If I had taken a step forward I would have fallen flat on my face. He muttered something, hauled the garment upwards and shortened the loop behind my neck. Then he doubled up the trailing apron front and tied the tapes around my waist. "Put those tins over there!" he growled.

The battered, brown, baking tins were all heavily greased and I arranged them neatly at the end of the largest of the wooden tables. The master baker went to his mechanical mixing bowl. He leaned over it, a carving knife in his hand, and cut a great swathe through the mound of dough. Thrusting in both arms he gave a quick heave and straightened up clutching a huge, floppy mass to his chest. Two quick steps and he slammed it down onto the wooden table near the tins. Silently he pointed at a pair of scales and weights, and beckoned for me to bring them closer. The dough was vaguely alive, slowly spreading and edging its way across the boards until Uncle Bob pushed it back into the corner of the table.

And then it began.

Huge hands grabbed the edge of the dough pulling it into a long thick sausage. Slash went the knife. A neatly cut lump was slammed onto the scales. They rattled, shook and settled – balanced at exactly the right weight. Another slash, another shuddering clatter of the scales and the piles of cut pieces of dough grew. Very, very occasionally the scales went down too hard and stayed down. Then Uncle Bob would mutter to himself and slice off pieces until the scales settled just right. Another time the weight might be too light, so there was more muttering and he would throw more dough onto the scales until they went down. There was a lovely, satisfying, thumping, clattering rhythm to it all.

Uncle Bob pushed the pieces of weighed dough into rows, counting them under his breath and then checking the line of waiting tins. One part of the process had clearly ended. He dipped his hands into a bowl of flour, slapping them together, and sending up a white cloud that drifted down his apron and settled on his boots. With a flick of the wrist a handful of flour was scattered over the worn wooden tabletop and carefully smoothed with sweeps of his hands.

"Right," he said. "I want those tins handy, and keep up!"

I was bewildered. Keep up? Keep up with what? I was soon to find out. Uncle Bob hitched up his sleeves, rubbed his dusty white hands together again and settled himself in front of the pieces of dough, with his legs set slightly apart like a veteran wild-west gun-fighter preparing for a fast draw.

"OK are you?"

I nodded, not knowing what to expect.

"Right then?"

Uncle Bob grabbed a piece of dough in each hand and banged them down on the table with a tremendous thump. He began rolling them into balls at startling speed. Each hand and wrist was moving rapidly in exactly the same way as if one hand was working in front of a mirror. The dough was punched, rolled, flattened, firmed, coaxed and cosseted. He stopped abruptly with a perfectly shaped uncooked loaf in each raised hand.

"Tins! Tins! Two tins," he shouted.

I came out of my admiring trance and grabbed two tins and pushed them towards him. Bang! Bang! The kneaded dough was slammed into each one and tucked smoothly into the corners.

"Put 'em over there.!" said Uncle Bob. "Come on. You'll have to move faster than that."

I took the two tinned loaves to the table near the oven and scampered back. He was already standing there scowling and pretending to be cross, holding aloft two more lumps of moulded dough. "Where's my tins? Where's my tins? Come on! Come on!"

I pushed two more tins within reach, grabbed the full ones and headed back to the table. I stopped in mid-stride; I would never keep up with him at this rate. I went back and pushed a semi-circle of empty tins within easy reach of the master baker. Uncle Bob's hands and wrists were now working automatically in perfect unison and at top speed. There was an approving look on his face as he watched me.

"Now you're learning!" he shouted. "Make a baker of you yet."

There was an echo of those words a few days later when I was out shopping with Mother. As usual it was slow progress, meeting people on street corners and talking, always talking. But I sensed that there was another topic of conversation: me, and for once I was spoken to directly in English. "Helping your Uncle Bob in the bake-house are you? Now that's nice. Want to be a baker when you grow up, then?"

Meaningful looks were exchanged. I had not given my future role in life much thought so I answered truthfully enough that I really did not know. Mother looked embarrassed and quickly ended the interrogation. For some reason 'helping Uncle Bob in the bake-house' had aroused some interest in the town.

My training as a baker continued on other visits. After the bread had risen in its tins it had to be baked. Uncle Bob used one of the long, paddle-ended poles hung from the ceiling to slide the tins into the farthest corners of the vast oven. It was shimmering with heat and sweat poured off his face. Every now and then he slammed the oven doors shut and wiped his forehead with his sleeve.

My job was to bring the different tins within working reach. Soon I was sweating, too, as the blasts of hot air shot out of the open doors. Once everything was safely packed inside and the doors tight shut Uncle Bob would check the temperature gauges and his watch. It was time to relax. He produced half a crown from his pocket. "Newsagents, on the corner. Tell him you've come for Mr. Ellis's usual."

I took off my apron, dusted myself down and did as I was bid. I was going shopping for my Uncle Bob. In my haste, at the top of the passage I bumped into a man walking along the pavement. The silver coin shot out of my hand and I watched transfixed as it rolled along the pavement and fell down a grating. Uncle Bob's money was lying on the windowsill of a basement window set way below pavement level. Half a crown was a horrible lot of money to lose. More importantly it was Uncle Bob's half crown. I could see it down there, but it was out of reach. I crept back to the bake-house and confessed.

To my surprise he was more amused that annoyed.

"Can you see it?"

"Yes," I said almost in tears.

"OK then."

He reached up and got one of the poles from its ceiling rack. He found a lump of dough left over from the weighing and moulded it around the handle end of the pole.

"You can reach it with that." he ordered.

For everyone in the high street I was an immediate object of curiosity. I was a miniature knight entering the lists, lance in hand, as I appeared with my paddle high above my head. I approached the grating. If it had been anyone other than my Uncle Bob who had put this weapon into my hands I would never have dared. The half crown was still there. I gingerly inserted the pole handle down between the bars. The sticky bit hovered over the half crown. Suddenly the sash window shot open, and a man's angry face was looking up at me from beneath the pavement. "What the hell do you think you're doing!"

I ran, dragging the pole behind me and ripping the dough off on the grating. It might have dropped onto the man's face for all I knew, I did not wait to find out.

"There was this man ..." I explained breathlessly to Uncle Bob. He listened patiently as he put the paddle back on its hooks.

"Get it myself," he growled.

I told Mother the whole story. "Stupid man! Tell him to get his own cigarettes in future."

A few nights later, under the dim gas light in Auntie Katie's parlour and with the shop bell the only break in the monotony, I thought it was time to make my contribution to the Welsh language. "I've learned some Welsh," I announced. "Uncle Bob has taught me."

Auntie Nell took a deep breath at the mere mention of his name. "And what's he been teaching you now, I wonder?" she said sighing wearily.

"He said I should tell you this, Auntie Nell."

I paused to make sure I had got it right and then carefully enunciated the phrase. Auntie Katie gave a startled cry and fled into the kitchen. Auntie Nell went bright red and Mother's eyes widened in shock.

On the way home I pleaded with her to tell me what I had said. "It was rude," she said. "Terribly, terribly rude."

"But what did I say? I want to know. "

"You told your Aunt Nell to go and scratch her ..." Mother hesitated. "Heels," she added.

"That's not rude," I protested.

"I don't want to hear any more about it. Just don't repeat anything your Uncle Bob tells you ever again – the stupid, silly man!"

So I asked a boy at school what I had told my Auntie Nell to go and do. No wonder they were all so shocked.

Eleven

My relationship with Uncle Bob had become a little guarded. I never mentioned the shock my Welsh pronouncement had caused and neither did he. On my next designated work day I arrived to see a queue filling the passage of Auntie Katie's shop. As the shop window was empty it was obvious they were all waiting for the bread to arrive. I quickened my step and hurried down the passage to the bake-house. Uncle Bob was waiting, beckoning impatiently and pointing to where I should stand behind one of the big tables.

He swung open the top oven doors and the heat struck us in the face. He peered into the brightly lit interior at a shimmering sea of swelling bread loaves. The door was swung shut again with a bang; sweat beaded his forehead and dripped into his eyebrows.

"When they're done," he growled at me. "You get them out of their tins, see, double quick, and you stack the tins there and put the bread over here. And watch your fingers 'cos everything is hot, see, bloody hot!"

He pondered for a moment and strode over to one of the rickety shelves on the wall where there was a neatly folded, Hessian flour sack. He tore it into strips and threw two of them at me. "Wrap that round your hands. I'm not having your Mother nagging at me for burning your fingers."

He partially opened the top oven door again for a quick look and the intoxicating smell of freshly baked bread flooded over us. Pulling down one of his poles from the ceiling rack he looked at me.

"Ready?"

I nodded. The oven doors were thrown wide open. In went the pole-paddle and two baking tins came crashing down on the table in front of me. The loaves spilled out crisp and golden. I stacked them at one end of the table and then picked up one of the tins. The heat seared through the Hessian 'gloves' so viciously that I dropped it with a yelp. Uncle Bob scowled at me. Wrapping part of his apron over one hand he expertly flicked one tin inside the other before throwing them both to the other end of the table with a clatter. So that was the secret – you did not take hold of the tins, you just flicked them around as quickly as possible. I stacked the two tins a little more neatly - my finger ends tingling – and waited.

"You OK?" asked Uncle Bob.

"Fine," I said, but I wasn't. My finger ends were on fire.

The oven door was swung open again, in and out went the long-handled paddle and the bread became a cascade. I worked on the loaves first, getting them all in rows before juggling with the hot tins. The oven door slammed shut and Uncle Bob, his face wet with sweat, was leaning on his pole and watching me. I had all the bread at one end of the table and all the tins stacked at the other. I had kept up with my Uncle Bob! I suspect there was a bit of a smirk on my face as our eyes met. My face must have said, 'How about that!'

I should have known better. He motioned to me to go behind the other empty table and the door of the furnace came open again. The long paddle swept in and out, this time at lightning speed. I was soon swamped by a mountain of tumbling, scalding hot tins. The loaves came in a torrent, a deluge piling higher and higher and all mixed up with the tins. The oven door was banged shut at last and Uncle Bob was grinning. "Come on! Come on! Keep up!"

This time he attacked the pile himself, pushing loaves three at a time into a huge wicker basket. "What's the time?" he demanded nodding towards the bake-house timepiece. This was an alarm clock that for some reason lived in an old biscuit tin with the clock face showing through a roughly cut hole in the lid.

"Ten o'clock," I said, as the huge wicker bread basket was expertly loaded with warm bread.

70

"You take this."

Uncle Bob produced a smaller wicker basket from under the table and quickly packed it - each loaf neatly slotted into place.

"Come on then! They won't wait all day."

He swung his basket of hot loaves up onto his shoulders and was off – ducking under the door arch and striding up the passage, with me at his heels nervously carrying my basket on my shoulder as he did. Out in the main street the queue had grown and there was a rustle of excitement and chattering as my Uncle Bob appeared. Here he was, a giant in a white apron bearing the daily bread, and there was I, the baker's apprentice, trotting along behind him.

We squeezed past all the customers in the shop entrance and the baskets were dumped on the counter. Auntie Katie shrank into a corner to make way as Uncle Bob rapidly stacked the bread along the shelves. I had to put my loaves on the shelves in the window and Aunt Kate stood behind me, carefully patting and re-arranging every loaf as I put it down. When my basket was emptied she went back to her pile of thin tissue paper whispering to the first customer in the queue, "Two white was it, and a brown?"

To reach the requested loaves she had to reach round the busy bulk of her brother - he not moving an inch to make way for her. Each loaf would be put carefully on top of the pile of tissue paper and slowly wrapped. Then she would softly whisper how much it was and put the money meticulously into the different compartments of the till drawer.

No-one was in a hurry. The arrival of the bread was a social occasion, a daily ritual, something to be savoured; so they waited, watched and chatted contentedly. But for us bakers, there was no time for chatter. Back we went for another load and I felt very important helping my Uncle Bob.

The baker's apprentice, trotting along behind him.

I was very disappointed with the war. When was it going to start? I had three rows of tiny flags all waiting on the edge of my war map in the front room. There were Union Jacks, French Tricolours and German Swastikas, and as yet they recorded no gallant advances. Sometimes the wireless said there had been shelling, and I would pore over my map and try and find a name.

"There, Auntie Nell. That's where it was, look …"

She would put on her glasses, "Humph!"

Clearly she was more concerned about what my map was doing to her wallpaper than the progress of the war.

All this inactivity bothered me. The Germans were not fighting and they were not bombing Newcastle either. So what was I doing here in Wales?

In the main street was a shop with gold lettering on the windows announcing that those within had been making and repairing shoes since 1880. The inside was very small and disappointingly bare. The long shelves behind the polished mahogany counter held a few shoe boxes on view, but there were scores of brown paper parcels each bearing a label.

"Is he in?" asked Mother.

"He's in the back," the old man behind the counter told her.

'The back' was a door at the far end of the shop. When we pushed it open we were in a room little wider than a corridor. Half the space was taken up with a bench littered with shoes; tools and more instruments for shoe mending festooned the walls. Occupying the rest of the cramped space was my Uncle William sitting on a high stool carefully shaping a piece of leather with a knife.

I was astonished. My Uncle William who had a very big car and lived in a very big house up on the hill and who was someone very important in the town was in fact a cobbler.

73

It was one long evening, when the wireless programmes were boring and Mother had lost patience with the coded Morse messages coming from the short wave on the radio, that I edged her into talking again about her life on her Northumberland island. I wanted to hear more about her war.

"We had a sea mine drifting near the rocks once," she said. "They said it would have blown all the glass out of the lighthouse if it had gone off."

This was more like it. "So what happened?"

"It drifted away." Mother laughed at my obvious disappointment.

"And the Zeppelin. Did someone shoot it down?"

"No. It flew away as well."

There was one English boy in a higher form at school, so in response to Aunt Nell's prodding about finding someone to play with I sought him out. But I did not like him. He seemed rough.

"Come round to my place," he said. "I've got some cap guns."

"I've got an anti-aircraft gun that fires pellets," I said.

"I'd like to have a go at that," he said a little too eagerly.

Even Mother was nervous about my new found friend and I was warned to be back home by eight o'clock. My new friend Jim did not give me his address; instead he said he would meet me in the square. I saw him standing by some railings in front of one of the big Victorian terrace houses.

"Down here," he gestured.

Behind the railings was a flight of stone steps leading down below pavement level. I could see a window and immediately had memories of Uncle Bob's half crown. Did people actually live under the pavement? These steps led to a narrow, paved space taken up with two smelly dustbins. Jim pushed a door open and I followed him inside only to be taken aback by the smell of cabbage, which I hated. The room was dim, with a baby's cot in one corner and a battered leather sofa with its stuffing protruding through several splits. A table was littered with mugs and plates, and surrounded by a weird assortment of stools and chairs. Around the grate was an iron fence covered with towels drying in front of the fire, and from the ceiling hung another contraption with still more washing. The floor was made of paving stones with one rug in front of the fire that looked as if it had been made out of bits of rag.

It was dim, because torn lace curtains covered the only window and the glass was only a few feet away from a brick wall. A tired looking lady dressed in black with her hair tied back in a bun was standing by a door into another room.

"Me Mam," said Jim curtly. The lady just stared at me and I wondered if she knew I was coming.

"Let's see the ack ack gun then." Jim pushed the dirty dishes to one side. I took Dad's precious present out of its carrier bag.

"Wow," said Jim snatching it off me and twirling the controls roughly between his fingers.

"How's it work?"

I showed him how to fit a cap into the breach block and a tiny rubber pellet in the tube behind it, cock the trigger, pull the lever and fire it. I had been using the pellets over and over again and they were getting loose in the firing tube. Instead of zipping off the ceiling it just popped out the barrel and bounced along the table.

"That's pathetic," Jim laughed. "Can't it do better than that? What a swizz!"

It was not a swizz! It was my special gun and my Dad had bought it for me. I reached out a hand to take it back. But he was not letting go.

"I can make it go. Give it 'ere." He half turned his back on me so I couldn't see clearly what he was doing. "Now it'll go. Watch this!"

Too late I saw what he had done. He had rammed four or five gunpowder caps into the breach instead of one.

"No!" I cried, but he pressed the trigger and it was like a real gun going off. The rubber pellet bounced off the wall and something else as well - half the breach mechanism. The extra charge had blown the working part of the gun to pieces.

Jim picked up the bits. "Bust! Can't have been very well made. Want to play snakes and ladders?"

"No!"

We played 'beg-o-my-neighbour' instead, with him crowing and snatching up the cards whenever he won. I wanted to go home, but first I wanted the toilet.

"Through there."

I went through a grim little kitchen, out of the back door and up some steps. At the end of a walled yard was a brick toilet with a stable door; inside there was a revolting smell. Torn squares of newspaper with a loop of string through the corners were hanging from a nail in the wall. I decided I did not want the toilet after all.

"Did you like playing with your friend," asked Mum.

"No, I didn't. He broke Dad's gun. And I don't want to see him ever again - even if he is English." I said it very loudly so Aunt Nell in the kitchen could hear me.

Twelve

The town was full of my relatives, which was probably the reason why we were always stopping to talk to people. Mother tried hard to explain who they all were, but I lost track of all the cousins who were either once or twice removed; where they had been removed to I could never work out. Being an only child would, I thought, have made family relationships simple, but here in Wales I learned they were hugely complicated. I decided to concentrate on the aunts and uncles and leave the cousins, moved or unmoved, to fend for themselves. This was because I met another aunt - a much more interesting one.

There was only one establishment in the town that could by any stretch of the imagination be regarded as a department store: Bon Marche. And even to me as a small boy it looked staid and old fashioned; the fancy wrought iron portico spanning the pavement failing completely to give it any sense of dignity or style.

The window displays were sparse, whilst inside a few frocks were displayed on headless wooden models making them look like ghosts haunting the guillotine. And the elderly assistants were almost as lifeless as the models. There was one thing here, however, that intrigued me: an overhead network of wires that ran from behind each of the counters to a glass-fronted little room at the rear of the store; here an elderly lady sat like an exhibit in a bird cage, knitting.

I was intrigued, but before I could work out what all this was for a woman appeared from one of the back rooms. She was not elderly, in fact she was rather glamorous, very smartly dressed and with luxurious, black, curly hair. She greeted Mother effusively and then looked at me. "This is him, is it? Good looking boy you got there, Helen. Break a few hearts that one!" She gave me a broad wink. "Come on. Give your

Auntie Mima a kiss. She doesn't bite."

A carefully made-up face came terrifyingly close to mine and planted a kiss on my blush-red cheek. She laughed before pulling a handkerchief out of her pocket.

"Put my mark on you, I have," she said wiping off the lipstick. "My God, that'll get the old hens clucking. Snatching them from the cradle now, she is."

Mother laughed and they were off chattering in Welsh. I was distracted by a sharp noise followed by a whoosh as something whizzed over my head. A small tin tube with a wheel on top was running along one of the wires I had noticed earlier. It disappeared into the glass fronted room. The woman inside reached up, unhooked the tube, emptied the contents on her desk, put some change back inside and re-hooked it to the wire. A lever was pulled and the tube came flashing back over my head towards one of the counters, where an assistant and a customer were waiting. It was an overhead railway system.

In the big Newcastle stores they had tubes let into the walls powered by compressed air for shooting the money around. I was so intrigued working out the different aerial routes that it took some seconds to realise that Mother and Aunt Mima were now talking in English.

"I don't know if he should go or not," said Mother. "What do you think?"

"He's got to learn about deaths and funerals sometime, hasn't he?" opined Aunt Mima. "And it's not as if he knew the man, is it?"

Aunt Mima looked at me and grinned.

Walking back from the store I asked Mother what all the talk had been about.

"It was about whether or not you should go to a funeral. He was a distant cousin of mine."

I did not inquire if he had been once or twice removed.

"I don't mind," I said cheerfully. "I've never been to a funeral."

Mother did her best to break up the nightly ritual of going to Auntie Katie's. Sometimes she would make no move to get her coat off the rack at the foot of the stairs when the usual time for the evening departure arrived. Aunt Nell would sense what was coming and there would be a weary, wounded tone in her voice. "You not coming tonight, Helen?"

And off Aunt Nell would go and I would be left feeling guilty, with disturbing visions of her getting lost in the black-out. "Will she be all right in the dark?"

"Uncle Bob will see she's OK."

"Uncle Bob?" I said.

"He follows her home at night if she's by herself. And so he should - he's her brother after all. But don't say anything. I'm pretty sure Nell knows he's there, but she pretends he isn't."

I decided my Welsh family was just weird.

When Mother and I we were in by ourselves for the evening and the Radio Times showed that there was nothing interesting on the wireless Mother would go exploring. She would turn the knob to the Short Wave Band and track the cursor cautiously across the dial past all those exciting names: Berlin, Vienna, Luxembourg - dark, mysterious, exciting sounding places. In our little back room in Wales we eavesdropped on the whole world. Often as she turned the knob there would be a rapid burst of Morse code and Mother would grab a pencil and start scribbling. Too often she flung down the pencil in disgust.

"Codes! Nothing but numbers! Everything's in code."

Sometimes she picked up innocuous messages in plain English, and to me all this was a marvel. How could anyone translate all that rapid bleeping into words, but Mother could. During the last years of the First World War she had been a radio telegrapher, despatching and receiving telegrams at a little post office in Northumberland, and she had never lost the skill.

My lighthouse keeper Grandfather had insisted that I learned Morse Code on the grounds that it might come in useful some day. My reward was a set of twelve children's encyclopaedias, which arrived at monthly intervals. It had been a whole year of delight and they became my most treasured possessions, each one fervently read as it arrived. The whole world was in those books waiting for me to delve into, but they were far too heavy to carry in our suitcases to Wales, so they had been left behind in Newcastle.

I felt that my window on the world had been closed, and worse still there was now a barrier of incomprehension between myself and the inhabitants of the tiny part of the world in which I lived. At first I tried to understand what was being said and what was going on around me, but then I gave up. I switched off and retreated within myself, which was an easy way of escape for an only child.

On the wireless before I went to school there was some dramatic news: the Germans were attacking. I rushed to my wall map with the names of the towns ringing in my head. Where were they? I had to get out my world atlas. The Germans were cheating! They were attacking in the wrong place. They had ignored the French Maginot Line, which was clearly marked on my map and were going round it through neutral Holland and Belgium. Neither of those countries was on my map, because they were not in the war; my map and my flags were all useless.

"That's not fair," I complained to Mother.

"It isn't, is it."

At school I did my best to avoid Jim and it was not too difficult. He was in a class above me and went round with an older group.

After our climb up the Garn little Dai sometimes sidled up to me in the playground to have a chat. I doubt if he had ever been out of the town in his life and he was curious about my 'big city' where they made ocean liners. He was full of questions.

One startled me. "Do they have any mountains in this Newcastle?"

I confessed that we had none, and then I remembered, "Oh yes we do, great big black ones." And I had to explain: "Slag heaps. From the pits. We had one near our school when we lived a bit further north."

"They're no good," said Dai contemptuously, obviously pleased that in one regard at least his town scored over my 'big city.'

"They're great for sliding down," I said. "We used to take cardboard boxes up to the top and slide down inside them. My Granddad went down with us once."

Dai's eyes widened. "Why did he do that?"

"He was visiting, picked me up from school and I said we were going down the slag heap, and he said he wanted a go. My Mam wasn't too pleased about it."

Little Dai thought for a while. "I think our Garn's better."

I gave the comparison a few second's reflection. "I think so, too."

Thirteen

My relationship with Uncle Bob was growing. When all the women were settled into Auntie Kate's parlour of an evening, and Uncle Bob had polished his dinner plate clean with a crust of bread, he would suggest we go for a walk. And so we embarked on a series of regular nocturnal wanderings, which took in every nook and cranny of the town and its surrounding fields and sand dunes. On our first venture we passed the Bon Marche store, all shuttered up.

"I met Aunt Mima there," I said.

"Did you now?"

"She's nice."

"Oh yes, she's very nice," said Uncle Bob with a chuckle. "You ask your Auntie Nell to tell you how nice Auntie Mima is."

I looked at him warily, and he playfully elbowed me in the ribs, nearly knocking me off the pavement. "Perhaps not, eh! Got you into enough trouble already."

And that made me curious about my Auntie Mima. There seemed to be something odd about all my relatives in this town. Uncle Bob and I walked along the harbour side in silence for a while. The tide had gone out leaving the boats sprawled helplessly on their sides in the mud. It was morbidly in keeping with the whole mood of this place - lost, cut off, at the end of the world.

"Going to the funeral are you?" said Uncle Bob suddenly.

I nodded.

"Big affair it'll be. They'll be all dressed up, you see. Chapel will stink of moth balls. Full watch and chain job, you bet. He was a grand old chap, though."

There followed a detailed account of my mother's, mother's dead second cousin - a tale full of anecdotes about the old man's days as a sea captain. "Always liked to be in charge, did Captain George. When the traffic got snarled up in the High Street he had to sort it out. Stood in the road he did, waving his arms about like a policeman. Mind you I've done that myself before the petrol rationing. Bloody chaos it was sometimes. Nearest policeman in Criccieth. Somebody had to do it."

I could just imagine my Uncle Bob in his apron and flour-spattered, black trousers waving his arms at startled motorists. They must have wondered what this apparition was in the middle of the road. I had a vivid imagination and I wondered if he stood on his bread basket to make himself more visible. Nobody could have ignored him then. I was about to ask when he said, "I'll look after you at the funeral. You haven't been to a Welsh funeral, have you? Jowl! They enjoy deaths better than weddings round here."

When the day arrived it was a shock to find out just how true this was. Auntie Nell came downstairs dressed all in black, and over her face was a veil with black dots that cast shadowy blotches all over her cheeks. It was an alarming sight. Fortunately Mother, anticipating that my reaction might be one of open-mouthed shock, had already warned me what to expect. Up in my bedroom I was told once again to say how smart Aunt Nell looked.

My sartorial contribution to the occasion was to wear a large, black, silk tie. It was taken out of a mothball-perfumed drawer and lovingly released from its tissue paper wrapping. I viewed it uneasily convinced that it must have belonged to Aunt Nell's long dead, minister husband. How many funerals had that tie attended, I thought mournfully, and now I was wrapping it and all its sad memories around my neck. I gave a little shudder.

When my aunt appeared, black from head to toe, I said dutifully, "You look very smart, Auntie Nell."

The head behind the veil nodded ever so slightly making the blotches on her cheeks do a disturbing little dance.

The three of us set off for the funeral on foot. Instead of going to the chapel, as I expected, we turned down a street of large terrace houses, each with a tiny strip of front garden cramped behind an iron railing and a gate. Aunt Nell sailed ahead of us, and went up the front steps of one of the houses and in through the front door, which was standing open. Mother and I followed, but then stopped. Our way was blocked by a coffin standing on trestles at the foot of the stairs. I recoiled slightly. There was a dead body in that box! Beyond the obstruction a woman's head appeared around an open doorway and an arm beckoned us forward. Aunt and Mother squeezed past the coffin, Aunt Nell with considerable difficulty, and then the woman noticed me.

"Men in the front room," she ordered. Mother was about to protest when suddenly Uncle Bob was standing by the door into the front parlour. "I'll look after him, Helen."

He pulled me gently into the front room, which was crowded with old, old men standing around uncomfortably in their best suits. The very oldest were squeezed onto a sofa, but the room was so crowded you could hardly see them. I was introduced and had to shake hands with everyone.

A great silence descended on the front room and we could hear the women in the backroom still talking. Uncle Bob was wearing a different suit that looked a little too tight, and for the first time he was wearing a collar, a stiffly starched affair supporting a black tie that looked as venerable as mine. He positioned himself behind me putting his large soft hands protectively on my shoulders.

"This bit won't take long," he whispered. I was glad to hear it, because there appeared to be no escape from this overcrowded, stuffy, little room except by edging past that coffin in the entrance hall. I glanced around. There were gloomy pictures on the walls of curly-headed children with angels smiling down at them.

My eyes constantly returned to that coffin; I had never been so close to one before and I was morbidly fascinated. The wood was very shiny and the brass handles glittered. Was the man inside still in his pyjamas, like when he died, or was he in his best suit, too? If so how did you dress someone when they were dead? And was it a 'watch and chain job' for him, too? My imagination was running riot.

A little man in a crumpled brown suit and a clergyman's collar squeezed himself uncomfortably in front of the coffin. He did not look like a real minister at all, even though he had a bible in his hand. He was half facing us in the front room and half looking through the door into the back room. He coughed. Silence fell and he began saying prayers in Welsh. Sometimes he turned his head towards us and sometimes towards the women in the back parlour. Both rooms joined in the prayers. By now I knew from the rhythm of the sounds when the Lord's Prayer was being said.

Uncle Bob was right - the service was brief, so brief that I wondered why we had all bothered to get so dressed up. A car horn pipped outside and four large men appeared adding dramatically to the congestion in the tiny passage. They squeezed round the coffin one of them catching his shoulder on a 'Mountains In The Rain' painting on the passage wall. Hurriedly one of the men put it straight.

Together they lifted the coffin off its trestles, but they could not swing it up onto their shoulders for fear of smashing the ceiling light. Two of them walked backwards carrying the coffin underhand, with the other two men struggling at the rear. The captain must have been a big man, for I could hear the bearers puffing and gasping at the weight. With them out of the house it was like a cork being released from a long-fermenting bottle.

"Let's get out of here." Uncle Bob pushed me forward. We all spilled onto the pavement and then spread out onto the road. I was amazed how many people had been squashed inside that house. Mourners were talking quietly in groups as the coffin was loaded into a hearse. That had not been too bad. What was all the fuss about?

Mother appeared with Auntie Nell and I heard her whispering to

Mother, "You go in the car."

"No we'll walk with Bob. You've got a bad leg. You go in the car."

So Auntie Nell got into one of the funeral cars with a very proud look on her face and I realised that it was not yet over. The hearse set off at a walking pace followed by the other cars, and then to my astonishment the rest of us followed walking in a long procession. And now I was perturbed, because people were lining the pavement and watching us go by, respectfully taking off their caps. I had never walked in a procession before with everyone watching me. Surely we were not going to walk all the way to that graveyard behind the mountain!

"Where are we going?" I whispered.

But all Mother said was, "Shhh!"

We were in fact going to the chapel. The service in the house had been for the immediate family; now the whole town was involved in the main event. I began to understand more fully what Uncle Bob had meant. We walked behind the hearse and saw the coffin carried inside the chapel. The building was full, even the upper gallery that ran around three sides of the building was packed with people staring down at us. The congregation got to its feet with a gentle referential clattering as the family occupied the front pews with much whispering and shuffling.

The service started and this time it was not short, in fact it went on and on. The minister prayed - his voice rising and falling like waves on a beach, with each crescendo came murmurs of approval. The minister left the pulpit and his place was taken by the cross-eyed man who ran the billiard hall - the one who had shouted, "No whistling," at my Dad. I guessed that he, too, was saying nice things about the man lying there in the coffin.

He was followed by another man and then another. A hymn was announced and we all got to our feet. A single chord on the organ was struck and a startling roar of voices rose in song, a roar so loud that the whole fabric of the chapel seemed to shudder. I could hear Mother's clear contralto and Uncle Bob's rumbling bass, all of them passionately singing their hearts out over that dead body in a box.

I did not know why, but suddenly I wanted to run away, to escape. I did not like all this fervour, noise and emotion, and I kept staring at that box and imagining a dead, sea captain inside. It was all so silly, but I could not help how I felt. I was gnawing my lip and close to tears. Uncle Bob had been glancing at me throughout the service and now his big arm came round my shoulder, and his hand gave my arm a friendly squeeze.

On and on the service went, more and more hymns were sung and the fervour grew and grew. Longer and longer prayers were punctuated with louder "Amens." And then it ended with a long, rustling silence that was like electricity pulsing in the air.

In that silence the coffin was carried outside and we all followed. Uncle Bob was talking quietly to Mother in Welsh. When he realised I was listening he lapsed into English.

"If Nell wants to make a meal of it, let her," I heard him say. "Graveyards are no places for children. He'll see his share of people put in the ground before he's done. There's no need for him to be starting now. The boy's had enough."

Mother was looking at me. "John you go with your Uncle Bob. I'll pick you up at Auntie Katie's later."

To Uncle Bob she said quite sharply: "You realise you'll miss the funeral tea."

"Oh what a shame," said Uncle Bob, but I thought I detected the ghost of a wink. "You'll pick him up from Katie's, then?"

Another procession was forming up for the march to the graveyard, but Uncle Bob and I walked away by another route. The few town people not at the funeral looked at us curiously, probably wondering why the baker and his assistant were in their best clothes – it not being Sunday. I thought it was a shame to be missing the funeral tea, but I certainly did not want to go to the graveyard. Uncle Bob meanwhile purposefully led the way into the town's only hotel.

"Hello, Mr. Ellis," said the girl receptionist politely from the dark little cubby-hole behind the front counter.

The manager appeared, "Hello, Mr. Ellis," he said respectfully.

There was much chattering in Welsh and the manager led the way down a dingy corridor with bits of wallpaper coming off the walls. Uncle Bob winked at me and we entered a very large room with tables laid out for tea.

"You'll be all right there," said the manager in English pointing to one of the tables. "And I'll get one of the girls."

When he had gone Uncle Bob whispered to me, "We're here early, because we've got to get the bread out, see? We haven't time to go to the interment. OK?"

"OK."

The manager brought not one, but two shy young waitresses out of the kitchen.

"Hello, Mr. Ellis," they chorused.

"Will sandwiches be all right for you, Mr. Ellis? There's ham," said one.

"And there's meat paste," said the other.

"Fine. And some cake, too, for the boy."

"Yes, Mr. Ellis."

They went back to the kitchen and returned with plates of sandwiches, and buns with a dab of pink icing sugar on top, and there was a large brown pot of very hot tea. In solitary splendour we had a grand funeral tea all to ourselves. I did not care that the rest of the funeral guests were singing mournful hymns in the graveyard behind the Garn. I was having the best tea I had had for ages.

Fourteen

The bake-house became my second home particularly at weekends. I found the unhurried ritual of bread-making strangely creative and satisfying. When the loaves were 'in,' lying plump, pale and snug in their tins, Uncle Bob pulled out his watch, did some mental calculations and said, "See you at two."

And I would either go home for something to eat or wander the streets while the bread baked.

When I did go wandering I usually ended up outside the ironmonger's shop with my nose against the glass: they had a wonderful display of knives. Mother had bought me a small pocket knife, but what I really wanted was a sheath knife. They were dangerous, Mother said, so I stared at the hunters' knives in their leather sheaths and dreamed that one day I would have one of those strapped to my belt.

After one hot Saturday's work in the bake-house Uncle Bob sprang a surprise. "Picnic on Sunday? You want to come? Ride in the car. Got some bread to deliver."

This last remark was accompanied by a wink, the meaning of which I did not understand at the time, but discovered later. Petrol for cars was rationed and strictly reserved for war work and essential deliveries - not for picnics. So in the unlikely event that we met an inquisitive policeman we would be 'delivering.' I then realised why Auntie Liz's husband William had thrown a lot of shoe boxes in the back of the car. He had been 'delivering' when he took us back to Aunt Nell's.

I had not been aware that Uncle Bob had a car and it turned out that he had not – it was a van with 'Ellis, Master Baker' written on the side. The next day it was parked outside the shop, but there was no sign of a picnic visible through the van's open back doors, only an empty bread basket. Uncle Bob was looking even smarter than he had been at the funeral; the trousers and jacket were the same, but they looked suspiciously as if they had been brushed and he had had a shave, because there was a fleck of red stained cotton wool stuck under his chin.

I sat in the front passenger seat my feet scuffing bits of paper and bread crumbs on the floor. Uncle Bob got in, swore under his breath and got out again and went into the house. The net curtains moved in the shop window and Uncle Bob's head and shoulders appeared gathering up the last few loaves left unsold in the window. He came back out and threw the bread unceremoniously into the basket in the back of the van. He winked at me as he got into the driving seat. Were they being 'delivered' or was that our picnic?

Off we went and I soon discovered that Uncle Bob's van was no ordinary vehicle; in fact it was as eccentric as its driver. While accelerating noisily in third gear there was a loud bang, which made me think the engine had exploded. But it was just the long gear lever giving a great jerk and falling out of position. This was followed by the engine roaring angrily as the vehicle slowed to a stop. Cursing loudly in Welsh Uncle Bob wrestled with the lever and, with brute force, rammed it into first gear. We took off again, up into second gear and then into third. Bang! It fell out again to the accompaniment of more Welsh curses.

"Rope! Rope!" Uncle Bob shouted pointing to a piece of heavy twine lying amidst the rubbish on the glove shelf in front of me. I picked it up and he grabbed it off me. The twine was already crudely knotted into a loop.

"Right you blighter, soon fix you," my uncle muttered in English. He hooked one end of the loop onto something under the dash board leaving the other end dangling. Up through the gears we went again. This time, when he reached third he slipped the loop of string over the gear lever to hold it in place. Triumphantly he accelerated through third gear giving me a thumbs-up sign. But then he had to unhook the string to get into fourth gear. Several times he forgot the string was there and bellowed what I took to be more Welsh profanities. It made for an interesting journey.

I watched his gear changing with fascination, wondering each time if he would remember the string. Eventually I made a suggestion, "Shall I hold it in gear for you, Uncle Bob?"

So I became assistant driver, as well as baker, holding the lever in place until a great fist jerked it out of my hand and pushed it into another gear. In this fashion we came to a village consisting of two rows of grey, pebble-dashed houses on either side of the road. Outside a house very much like Auntie Nell's Uncle Bob stopped and pipped his horn. The door opened and a lady came out wearing a very girly summer frock and carrying a basket. She was old and to my critical young eyes almost witch-like, with a long thin wrinkled face dominated by a big nose. The face broke into a cheerful grin disclosing some disturbingly large teeth, but for all that she was very jolly and friendly.

"This is my friend Mrs. Roberts," said Uncle Bob.

"Irene! Irene!" she cried. "Call me Auntie Irene! John is it? Helping Bob at the bake-house, aren't you?"

I nodded, not knowing what to make of this surprise extra person at our picnic; at least there was now the prospect of food. Auntie Irene was carrying a basket, which looked promisingly large and heavy. With her arrival I was banished to the back of the van and I made myself comfortable on an old car tyre while clutching the picnic basket on my knees.

"Mind my fishing rod back there," said Uncle Bob. And we were off, Uncle and Auntie laughing and chatting in the front and me hanging on for dear life in the back. Who, I wondered, was Mrs. Roberts?

Out in open country in a dry-stone walled country lane the van stopped and I had to get out and open a gate. Uncle Bob drove the van into the field. We bumped riotously over the grass and down a slope with everyone being thrown about inside and Irene shrieking with laughter and complaining loudly. We stopped at last amongst some trees alongside a shallow river where the water meandered around shoals of pebbles and eddied gently into darker, deeper pools. It was a wonderfully peaceful spot for a picnic.

"You silly, silly man," cried Irene in English when the van finally stopped. "What you drive like that for?"

"Never grown up, he has," she said to me.

This was certainly a new Uncle Bob, someone mischievous with a sly grin on his face. As my new-found aunt laid out a rug and set out the picnic on the grass the cheerful banter went on between them. Uncle Bob did not offer to help. Instead he took out his fly-fishing rod, and after carefully assembling it beckoned me to follow him to the river's edge, where the brown shadows of trout were lurking. Their mouths were just breaking the surface and sending widening rings of ripples across the water as they took some unsuspecting fly.

From an old tobacco tin stuffed with what appeared to be fragments of a blanket Uncle Bob selected a brightly coloured artificial fly and showed me how to fasten it to the line. Rubber waders came out of a box in the back of the van, great black things that reached up over his thighs; he walked slowly into the river making scarcely a ripple.

I took off my shoes and socks and paddled after him wobbling uncomfortably on the stones. Pulling me in close beside him he flicked his rod and the line went in a great loop, dropping the fly on top of one of the brown, shimmering shadows. To my astonishment he caught three fish in quick succession, all small, which he unhooked with surprising gentleness and put back into the water. I was given the rod to try, but caught nothing.

With my feet freezing I waded back to the bank to help with the picnic. Irene had a towel, "Loves his fishing, he does," she said rubbing my frozen feet briskly. "Waste of time, really. Never eats them. I think

94

he just likes to paddle." And we both laughed.

We had our picnic – thick spam sandwiches well laced with tomato sauce and more 'sticky bread.' There was a lot of laughing and chattering in Welsh and I got the impression these two knew each other very well indeed. While Uncle Bob stretched out on his back puffing his pipe, Aunt Irene took me for a walk along the river bank pointing out the different wild flowers and birds as we went. I decided that I quite liked my Auntie Irene, even if she did look like a witch in a girly summer frock.

We packed up the picnic, reloaded the car and went back to her house. There she gave me a hug and Uncle Bob carried the picnic basket into the house. "Won't be a minute," he said, leaving me waiting by the van.

In fact he was in the house for ages and I could hear them inside laughing and chattering. When he reappeared he was obviously in a very good mood. He was singing to himself, and as we drove back to town he had also mellowed to the leaping excesses of the van's third gear. A new system was in operation. He simply ignored the gear altogether - roaring along in second gear and then crashing the lever straight into top. We arrived outside Auntie Nell's house and Uncle Bob went all quiet and grown up again.

"I enjoyed that." I said to him. "Thank you very much."

"Tins tomorrow, ten o'clock? Could do with some help."

"Right."

He nodded.

"Your Auntie Nell…" he began. "Don't mention Mrs. Roberts to her. The two of 'em don't get on, you see. So best not. Just you and me on the picnic, OK?"

I was sharing secrets with my Uncle Bob! "Of course."

"Did you have a good time?" Mother asked. "You must be starving. I bet he never thought to take along any food."

"We had a picnic."

"Picnic, picnic?" said Auntie Nell, her ears twitching in the kitchen. "That man's never cut a slice of bread in his life, never mind made a picnic."

I blushed hotly. Already I was in danger of betraying our secret. Fortunately Aunt Nell was out of sight in the kitchen.

"Katie will have made it for them," said Mother.

"Humph!" came the voice from the kitchen. "Typical that is. Treats her like a slave he does. He'd never think of taking her out on a picnic, oh dear me no."

Nothing more was said so I did not have to tell Mother about yet another new aunt.

Fifteen

Father came for a few days' holiday. He was hardly off the train before I was badgering him to climb the 'biggie' – Snowdon. Despite Aunt Nell's sharp disapproval, out came the maps and the timetables. Mother, who had gone very quiet about the whole adventure, was to be dropped off in a village *en route* to the mountain and spend the day there with some distant cousin. We were to walk up the mountain, come down on her side and meet her there. It did not look far on the map.

We left Mother in a tiny village, which consisted of a handful of grim, slate-topped houses while Father and I went on to Llanberis by bus.

Our mountaineering dress was basic: sports jackets and flannels and two rolled up mackintoshes in case it rained. The rest of our 'equipment' in two small haversacks consisted of sandwiches, bottles of water and a map.

In Llanberis Station the mountain steam train was in hibernation for the duration of the war and the rail track stood empty, yet clearly pointing the way. All around us were mountains with their tops covered in cloud. They looked worryingly hazy and I concluded that there was not going to be much of a view. But Father was full of determined enthusiasm, as usual. Off we went 'sleeper-ending' as he called it – walking on the edge of the wooden sleepers that supported the railway line. If a train could ride up a mountain so could we, said Dad.

The surrounding hills looked cold, barren and uninviting. We marched one behind the other and very soon the low cloud closed in around us and we could not see the other mountains. I was beginning to have grave doubts about the whole adventure. Our horizon was only a few yards in front of us, made up of barren rock and a railway line that continuously faded into a cloudy nothingness ahead.

Father felt the need to consult his map. My nervousness about his map-reading abilities remained, but the presence of the rail track was firm and reassuring, and it was clearly marked on the map. What worried me was the vague, dotted line that continued from the end of the railway and marked the path down the other side.

On we tramped. The ground on either side of the track was starting to fall away quite steeply and the gradient of the railway line had also increased. The air was cold, and I sensed that we were walking along a narrow ridge, but still I could not see a thing. On and on we walked, with me staring at the haversack on Dad's back until I felt almost mesmerised. I was cold, bored and vaguely frightened all at the same time. Would the railway never end?

And then at last, at long last, a shape appeared out of the mist - a drab, dismal, disappointing concrete building on a tiny patch of level ground. The track ended at a set of buffers and alongside a short platform. We had walked to the top of the world. Why had we bothered? What a disappointment it was. There was no breathtaking panorama stretched beneath our feet, in fact there were no views at all. Our ghostly, cloud-wrapped world consisted of this one tatty building wreathed in mist. And inside it was not much better. It was like a factory canteen with its concrete floor, scruffy chairs and tables, and a large tea urn on a serving counter; at least inside it was warm. There were two other inhabitants, one behind the counter and the other perched on a stool in front of it. They gaped at us as if we were creatures from another planet.

"Two teas please," said Dad briskly.

It took some moments for the request to sink in and when it did the man behind the counter simply pulled the tea urn over at an extraordinary angle and coaxed out enough liquid to fill two mugs, and handed them over.

"You know there's no train," he said accusingly.

"I know. There's a war on," said Father cheerfully.

Neither man was amused. They looked at one another and spoke in Welsh. For a moment I thought something was going to be added in English, but they thought better of it, and reluctantly went back to their own conversation.

We drank our tea in silence while Father got out his map yet again. He decided he needed help and took it over to the men and laid it out on the counter.

"How do we get onto that path?" he said pointing.

The man in charge of the urn nodded towards the exit at the other end of the canteen. "There's a path marker outside."

The other man broke into an animated exchange in Welsh. The man behind the counter just shrugged his shoulders so the customer addressed us both in English. "I'd go back down by the railway if I were you," he said with a pronounced Welsh lilt in his voice. "'Specially with the boy."

"We're meeting the wife down the other side," said Dad. "It's a proper path, isn't it?"

"I suppose it is. But it's a bit dodgy like."

"We'll be all right. We've been up mountains before."

"Have you now," said the man uncertainly.

I was now keenly aware of the man's concern and I was not reassured by Dad's air of confidence. We had only been up one mountain and I kept thinking of that bog into which he had walked us.

The two men exchanged glances. They reminded me of a horror film I had seen where two characters in an ale-house try to warn travellers of evil ahead.

"Right then, off we go," said Dad.

I did not relish going out into the cold again, but neither did I want to stay in this vaguely unfriendly place. Outside the mist was even thicker, the air colder, and I had the terrifying feeling that I was perched on top of the world - even though I could see nothing. But the man was right – there was a signpost pointing to a path, but we could only see a few yards along it, because of the cloud.

Please, please let's go back by the railway, but what about Mother waiting in that village? I followed in Father's footsteps as the path grew narrower and jagged pieces of rock rose up on our left hand side. There appeared to be nothing to our right at all apart from cloud and mist, and I instinctively edged to my left touching the rock with my hand for reassurance.

Then that hand hold disappeared and there was just the path with nothing on either side. My heart started to beat and my mouth went dry. Nothing, but this narrow path under our feet and on either side - what? Looking down I could see nothing, but that was no comfort for it just set my imagination churning out nightmares. We were up in the sky, lost in our own silent world. We might never see the earth again. Were my feet only inches away from ... what? I could feel my heart beating faster, and despite the chill I was sweating. There was nothing pleasurable in climbing mountains, I decided. It was pointless. It was dangerous. And it was frightening.

There was an upsurge of cold air, which suddenly swirled the mist away. I could see. And it was worse than any of my imaginations. Frozen to the spot, I gasped with shock. We were walking along the edge of a narrow escarpment. To our right was a vertical drop of thousands of feet to a sinister black lake. And my feet really were inches away from the edge. If there had been any breath in my lungs I would have screamed. I looked away and got another shock. We had another twenty yards to go along this knife edge escarpment before the ridge flattened out.

Dad had stopped, too, for a moment. "Keep going," he called. "Don't look down. Keep going. Follow me."

I edged forward after him What if I fell off? What if he fell off? That big black lake far down below was looking at me, beckoning me.

"What are you doing up there?" it seemed to be saying. "Come down here to me."

I dragged my eyes away and fastened them instead on Dad's feet slowly pacing along the path. My heart was still thumping, my forehead still sweating, and I was breathing quickly through my mouth like a thirsty little dog.

"Don't look down," called Dad over his shoulder. "Not far now. Keep going. Don't look down."

There was no need for that advice. I did not dare look down again, because one glance had been enough. That lake was etched into my brain forever. We walked slowly, each step a triumph of willpower over sheer terror. What if the path crumbled and gave way? How long would it take for me to fall all the way down and disappear for ever into that black water? My mouth was parched. I wanted a drink, but there was no way I could stop and get one from my haversack. If I stopped I knew I would never move again. My eyes were fixed on Father's feet - when they moved I moved.

We reached the end of that hellish escarpment and the path broadened out. My heart was still beating rapidly, but the worst was over. Down the other side of the mountain we went, it was steep and rough, but not as terrifying as that crest. I forced myself to admire the views that appeared, and we walked in complete silence until we reached a road. Only then did I look back at that monstrous 'thing', with its head wrapped in cloud, and I shuddered. That mountain had scared the wits out of me. Dad looked at it, too, and gave my shoulders a friendly little shake.

"Well done," he said.

And he stopped, lost for words. I bit my lip and felt guilty.

"But I was frightened," I whispered. "Very, very frightened."

"Course you were. But you kept going didn't you? That's what matters. You did it!"

I nodded my head vigorously, I was close to tears.

"Dad."

"What?"

"I don't think I want to go up any more mountains - not for a bit anyway."

"Quite right. Been there, done that. So now where are we?" And out came the map again. To my intense surprise we had arrived where we wanted to be.

With our spirits rising we headed down a country road and came to the village where Mother and her cousin were waiting for us. Waiting for us they most certainly were, and in a high state of anxiety. Mother's cousin knew all about Snowdon and had told Mother that the route we had taken was highly dangerous even in good weather. She got Mother into such a state that they were about to call the police when we wandered jauntily into the village.

Over tea and on the bus back home there was a very strained atmosphere, with Mother constantly demanding if I was all right. I lied unconvincingly and felt sorry for Dad. I had pushed him into doing it and our relationship changed subtly as a result - now we were fellow conspirators.

"We won't forget that in a hurry will we?" he whispered to me when Mother was not listening. "

"Never ever," I said.

Sixteen

The summer blossomed, the distant mountains stood out sharp and clear against the blue sky, looking as crisp as picture postcards. And in the soft sunshine the town quietly, almost furtively, laid hold of me. There were no soulless housing estates, no litter-strewn slag heaps, no factories, no pits and no aircraft droning overhead. Instead there were open fields, distant hills and sand dunes to explore. Here I felt I could breathe. People still talked Welsh over my head, but at least they smiled and nodded at me as they did so. And whenever I wore my oversized apron and carried the bread into the shop behind Uncle Bob the customers would nod and grin, and Auntie Katie would look at me wistfully with her sad, sad eyes. Sometimes she would pat my arm with a touch so light that she might have been a ghost, and yet I never once saw her smile, really smile and I certainly never once heard her laugh.

In the bake-house I got to know every tin, every bowl, and every bent and twisted little knife each with its own purpose, either for opening sacks or slicing patterns into the tops of the 'specials.' And the smell of freshly baked bread, golden and brittle-crusted wormed its way into my soul. I would open the door into the bake-house and that smell would hit me fresh and exciting every time, and there would be Uncle Bob, sleeves rolled up, flour flecking the hairs on his massive forearms like frost on a bush, nodding at me to come in.

More and more at the family gathering in Katie's back parlour Uncle Bob would push his empty plate to one side and growl: "Walk?" And we would go off on another meander down country lanes and across fields, often arriving on a beach with the waves endlessly churning the pebbles in the semi-darkness. There was one green lane, which was haunted by bats, a lane so overgrown with trees that in places it looked like a long, shadow-speckled tunnel.

"You watch this now," said Uncle Bob putting a grubby, off-white handkerchief on top of his hat - a disreputable affair full of rips and tears from storing spare hooks and 'flies' when he went fishing. The bats came swooping down the lane twisting, turning and diving. I ducked as the tiny black shapes hurtled towards us, whilst Uncle Bob stood there like a lighthouse assaulted by seagulls and never flinched.

And when there was no Uncle Bob to walk with I would wander the town by myself often ending up on the Garn, sitting on the concrete survey triangulation column on the top, looking out to sea and at the distant mountains. And sometimes, but only sometimes, I would look down at that graveyard behind the town. Even in summer sunshine it disturbed me. It just lay there, saying nothing, doing nothing - waiting.

And then one morning after reading a letter over breakfast Mother looked up at me, "John, I think we should be going home, don't you?" And I did not know what to say.

"It's not fair on your Dad," she said quickly. "He misses you."

I missed him, too, but now my thoughts were churning. Did I want to go back to the streets of that big, black town, with its great iron bridges over *The Tyne, the Tyne, the coaly Tyne the Queen of arl the rivers'* as Dad used to say in an exaggerated Geordie accent? There would be no more mountains; no more fields strewn with rocks, bracken and gorse; no more bake-house; no more Uncle Bob. I did not have time to brood, the next day we packed.

Auntie Nell hugged me and I was astonished to see tears in her eyes. Auntie Katie hugged me, too, pushed me brusquely away and ran into the back parlour without saying a word, slamming the door behind her. Slowly, by myself, I went down the passage through the houses to the bake-house and pushed open the stable door, wondering whether I would ever make this journey again. Uncle Bob was standing behind the big, baking table both hands rhythmically moving backwards and forwards over two pieces of dough.

Neither of us said anything for ages. "You going then?" he said at last. And all I could do was nod.

He wiped a flour-covered hand across the front of his apron. "Well then," he said holding it out for me to shake. My hand disappeared inside his, and again I was surprised how soft and gentle it was. "You'll come back and see me, will you?"

From beneath the wildly sprouting, spiky eye-brows I was being closely watched.

I nodded. "Holidays," I said.

The word was escaping from my throat in a strangled whisper. I did not trust myself to say any more without bursting into tears. We both stared at each other in silence. He picked up the two moulded pieces of dough and slammed them into the tins. Bang! Bang! There was something terribly final about it, like two rifle shots.

"Off you go. No point in hanging about. You come and help me next time you're here, right?"

Uncle Bob waved a dismissive hand in the direction of the door and I fled stopping only in the seclusion of the passage between the houses. There in the shadows I burst into tears and sobbed and sobbed.

So we went back to Newcastle, but not for long. Soon the furniture van was outside the house and again all my books and toys disappeared into the same old tea chest that was always mine when we moved. It was the seventh time we had changed house and my sixth school awaited me. Father was always trying to get promotion, and this time he had been given a place with the London and North Eastern Railway, at York. Once again our tired furniture was dragged into the shabby light of day and dumped into the back of a huge van, soon to be joined by folded carpets and rolled up linoleum strapped vertically against the van walls.

My new home was a tall thin Victorian terrace house, one of a row climbing up a suburban hill in York. The entrance hall was narrow and dark, an instant gloomy reminder of that coffin-blocked corridor in

Wales. But my spirits rose as I explored. This house had an attic, reached by a steep staircase hidden behind a door on the top landing. And that attic, I was told, was mine, all mine. One of the removal men struggled up the narrow staircase with my tea chest in his arms. He dumped it on the bare floorboards in the middle of my new kingdom.

"Grand playroom," he said looking round.

I stood on the tea chest to reach the skylight and opened it with a push-out iron bar. There was no sea, no mountains, no green fields, just the roofs of scores of other houses. I was hemmed in by slates, tiles and chimney pots. I opened my tea chest and soon had everything strewn all over the floor. Now I had some space of my own, which was far better than the corner of Aunt Nell's front room. Perhaps things would not be so bad after all.

I was called down into the kitchen for our first meal in our new house – corn beef and chips. Our two jam jars each half full of sugar and labelled John and Dad had been unearthed from a packing case and were on the table beside the tea pot. This was our weekly sugar ration. Dad and I were always in competition to see who could make it last the longest; he always lost - his jar was always empty long before the week was up. Mother did not have a jam jar.

"My ration goes into the cooking," she would say, but I suspected that most of it went into our jars.

Once back from the safety of Wales, Mother made me very conscious of the fact that we had returned to a war zone. She found a secure place for the family emergency food store – the built-in cupboard alongside the fireplace in the living room. It was a well established fact that under the stairs or beside the chimney breast was the safest place to be if there were any bombing. So into the chimney breast cupboard went all the tins that Mother had hoarded in boxes in our old house in Newcastle.

There was fruit, mainly plums, which Mother had preserved in Kilner jars - special glass jars with metal clips securing the lids. These had to be regularly checked to make sure the contents had not 'gone off.' White mould inside the jar was the warning sign and caused great concern. But even then the contents were never wasted. The layer of white fungus was scraped off and thrown away, and the rest of the plums boiled and eaten with custard or even rice when available. This was never popular, because the plums were always sour and hard decisions had to be made – was it to be sweet plums or drinkable tea? Looking in that store cupboard I always thought we could live on the contents for months as long as we did not lose the tin opener. On Sundays it was raided for the week-end treat - a tin of pineapple chunks or a mixed fruit salad. Father and I would have mock squabbles over who would have the red bits of cherry in the salad.

At the bottom of our long, narrow garden was something I had not seen before, a grim reminder that we really had moved closer to the war. It was our own air raid shelter - a brick-walled, windowless hut with a flat, concrete roof and slatted bench seats supported on iron brackets. When Dad and I explored inside we found a box of candles, several of which had been used, and some spent matches. That set us thinking - the previous house occupants had obviously spent time huddled in here. We really had moved closer to the enemy and that very night in our new house the sirens sounded. The howling, wailing sound, rising and falling had a terrible urgency about it. Mother and Father were out of bed, I was half asleep and Mother wrapped a dressing gown round me and we all rushed down the garden to the shelter, in our slippers. We crouched in our brick box in total darkness, shivering in our pyjamas and dressing gowns.

"I've not got any damn matches," said Father.

"You should have left some in here," said Mother crossly.

"I'll go get some."

But there was the pulsating drone of aircraft passing overhead.

"You'll do no such thing."

So we sat and shivered for nearly an hour with aircraft passing overhead, but no bombs fell. The siren sounded again, the long, sustained howling note of the All Clear and back to bed we went. I shivered long after I had got warm. There was a war on after all. Those were Germans flying over us. Quiet, peaceful Wales was already becoming an idyllic, nostalgic memory.

My new headmaster wore a mortarboard and walked around with a cane hooked into his jacket pocket and half hidden under his gown.

"Keeping my little friend warm," he would say, patting the instrument affectionately.

We were terrified of him. I was once again on my educational roller-coaster. The headmaster had decided that he was personally going to take us all for maths. To assess our abilities, he announced that there would be a mental arithmetic test of twenty questions. I hated maths and I was in such a state that I even had difficulty in writing my name on the exam paper. And when he began sweeping imperiously up and down the classroom in his cap and gown and suddenly announced, "Question one!" my brain stopped.

He was into the second question before I understood the first. The second question I understood, but I was concentrating so hard on working it out that I did not even hear question three. And the panic got worse as the blank spaces grew. The headmaster gathered up the papers and returned to his desk to read them. I had never heard such a silence or felt such fear in a classroom. He looked at the papers, and he looked at us. He shuffled and patted them into a neat pile and then slowly tore them in half and threw the bits into a waste paper basket. He walked out without saying a word. Obviously the day of judgement was to come.

At home we were getting bored and annoyed with the nightly air raid warnings. The sirens would wail and we would troop down to the shelter carrying blankets and matches, but nothing happened; there was just the droning of aircraft high overhead. From the news on the radio we learned that these were German bombers heading for the docks in Liverpool – they were not interested in us.

On the radio, Lord Haw Haw with his 'Germany Calling' broadcasts kept us informed of the destruction the planes were wreaking. Mother was incensed and got Father to write a letter to the Ministry of Information saying they should answer Lord Haw Haw back.

At that time Father was suffering from an outburst of boils and Mother was convinced that it was because of the poor quality of the National Loaf we were eating. So while Father wrote to the Ministry of Information Mother wrote to the Radio Doctor at the BBC.

To my astonishment we got a reply from both of them. First, written on imposing headed paper, came the response from the Ministry of Information: the Government would not give publicity to German propaganda by replying to it directly. And then the Radio Doctor…

On one of his regular morning broadcasts his avuncular voice assured us that the National loaf did not cause boils and was in fact highly nutritious. For boil sufferers, like my Dad, he advised a balanced diet with plenty of fresh green vegetables. I was hugely impressed, but Mother was not; she felt this was a slight on the quality of the food she provided for her family. Henceforth the Radio Doctor was viewed with suspicion and doubt.

The radio was, nevertheless, our world. When the BBC announced that we had bombed two important German ports in the Baltic, we all shouted, "Hurrah!" We were thinking of what they were doing to Liverpool. Lord Haw Haw said it was a barbaric raid on two historic towns of no military value whatsoever, and that the Fuehrer was incensed.

"Hard cheese!" we gleefully shouted at the radio. In his nasty,

Keeping my little friend warm.

sneering, toffee-nosed voice Lord Haw Haw said that the Fuehrer had ordered reprisals. If the RAF bombed Germany's historic towns then the Luftwaffe would bomb historic towns in England. And, he added, he had a little list. Even when Canterbury was bombed and Exeter it never dawned on us that Herr Baedeker in his guide book of England had given York star rating.

Meanwhile I was getting to know the old city well and I found a way of getting to school on foot that beat the bus. If I ran across the stray and down a path past the convent school I could climb up the steps onto the medieval city walls. Sprinting along the ramparts, looking down on the city as I went, I was at school in no time. And I could make it back home for lunch in twelve minutes, trotting all the way.

This route stood me in good stead on my third morning when the headmaster thought his cane had been kept warm long enough and needed exercise. He decided to have a purge on late-comers. I sat smugly in class while half the school, all late-comers, queued up outside for 'one on each hand', with the head and another master brandishing their canes in unison at the school front door.

Seventeen

And then came the night…

There was no siren just a whistling noise that grew louder and louder followed by a terrifyingly loud bang. The ground heaved and my bed shook. "What the bloody hell was that?" I heard Father shouting in the bedroom next door.

"It was a bomb," my mother said crossly. "What did you think it was? Get John, now!"

It was the middle of the night and we had all been fast asleep, but we knew the drill. We rushed downstairs grabbing the three tin hats that were hung on the coat rack in the hall.

In the semi-darkness a debate began about where we should go.

"What's it to be? The shelter or stay in the house?"

"I'd feel a lot safer in the shelter, if we could get there." Dad's voice had a strange calmness about it that did not sound quite real.

"What if we're caught out there in the garden….?"

By then I was too terrified to care where we went.

Another long whistling noise followed by a thump and a shudder decided us. We flung ourselves into the alcove by the chimney breast in the front room, huddled so close together our tin helmets rattled.

A pulsating droning in the sky grew louder. Somehow we knew these planes were not going to pass over - they were coming for us. Always cursed with a vivid imagination, I saw them as angry bluebottles closing in on a corpse lying in the road. More bombs fell. They were coming in 'sticks' now, with a short pause between each explosion. Bang! Bang! Bang! Bang! Our front room lit up in brilliant pulses, for all the world like a photographer's flash-bulbs going off in quick succession. The windows shook so violently all I could do was to hold my breath and pray that the sticky tape recommended in the air raid precautions manual would save us from flying splinters if the windows did shatter. Then in the midst of this chaos the air-raid siren sounded.

"Thank you very much for telling us!" Father shouted. "Woken up at last have you? About bloody time!"

"There's no need to swear Bill," I heard Mother saying softly.

The aircraft noises came and went and so did the explosions, thankfully most of them sounding some distance away. I knew I mustn't cry, but I started to shiver and I could not stop. My mother's arms came round me. Suddenly there was a lull, startling in its contrasting silence, and there was another quick family debate.

Again, Father's voice had a false calmness about it. "Should we make a dash for the garden shelter or stay indoors?"

There was fear in Mother's voice, "What if they come back?"

"I'd feel happier if ..." began Father, but before we could decide what to do that distant droning started again - another wave of aircraft was moving in. We stayed where we were in a huddled heap on the front room floor, cowering in the chimney breast alcove furthest from the window. We shivered, we waited and I think Mother was praying. Explosions began again.

The whistling sound of one particular bomb began faintly a long way away, and grew louder and louder until it became a wild scream threatening to burst our ear drums.

"It's coming down our chimney!" I cried.

We clung to each other and waited...

It passed over us. There was a dull, heavy thump, but, strangely, miraculously, no explosion. We were still alive, but the sense of relief did not last long. A plane roared low over the house and there was a violent rattle of machine gun fire. I was sure the bullets were pinging off our roof.

"That's our Spitfires," said Dad encouragingly. "Our lot's after them now! Soon be over."

I was not convinced. I was imagining some evil-faced Hun up there in the sky, with his sinister black-leather flying helmet and goggles, gleefully spraying us with machine gun fire, because he had run out of bombs.

Even with Mother and Father crouched protectively over me I did not feel at all like cheering. Perhaps Dad was right. The frequency of the explosions lessened and the aircraft noises faded.

It became ominously quiet and at long last came the plaintiff wailing of Moaning Minnie, the All Clear siren. It was all over and we were still alive. But what had those midnight raiders who had descended on us out of the darkness done to our town? What chaos was out there waiting for us?

Tentatively we opened our front door and went out into the street not knowing what to expect; dark figures in dressing gowns were emerging from other houses. We all met in groups in the middle of the road and from the vantage of our small hill looked down towards the city centre about a mile away. Lurid orange flames were glowing and dancing against the dark night clouds, while other smaller fires speckled the entire horizon; grim black smoke was boiling upwards.

Our next door neighbours were two spinster sisters, Mother called them Gert and Daisy, after the comedians on the radio. They were peeping out of their front door like timid kittens, but when they saw us all in the street they, too, emerged. One of them clutched a bottle of whisky as they joined us in the middle of the road. It was odd seeing all our sedate neighbours in their dressing gowns and pyjamas, some of the women had their hair in curlers.

It took some minutes for Gert and Daisy to realise what they were looking at, but when they did they started wailing and waving their arms in the air and crying, "York's burning! York's burning!"

"Drunk!" said Mother in disgust.

Drunk or sober we all helplessly watched the fires, wondering what to do. The adults were talking in low voices, as if frightened that the Germans might hear them and come back.

"I wonder if they got the Minster?"

"What are they bombing us for?"

"We've got no factories here."

"Bloomin' Germans."

Then there was a plaintive woman's voice, very quietly spoken. "I wonder how many have been killed."

All went quiet, and another woman said sharply, "Shush, the boy." They were all looking at me in the semi-darkness.

"It's getting very cold out here," said Mother briskly. "What we need is a nice hot cup of tea."

I was ushered back into the house, the kettle was put on and the tea cups brought out. And comforting normality returned.

"Put in plenty of sugar, John," Mother ordered. "Sweet tea is good for shock." I did as I was told though there was not much of my weekly sugar ration left in my own, personal jam jar. "Now drink up and get yourself back to bed. You've got to get up for school in the morning."

"School!"

It was four o'clock in the morning! We had just been bombed by the Germans. And I was expected to go to school?

That was definitely not fair.

Over breakfast, a few hours later, it seemed like a bad dream. Had it really happened? And Mother was having second thoughts?

"Do you think it'll be safe? Should he really be going to school?" she asked Father.

"Business as usual! I'm going to work, he's going to school."

So off I went. The first thing I noticed at the bottom of our hill was that the road to the shops had been blocked off. A notice read 'Unexploded Bomb'. It was probably the one I thought was going to come down our chimney. I looked down the side street near the primary school. Some of the houses had collapsed, spilling bricks and torn timbers right across the road. Air Raid Wardens were climbing all over the rubble digging holes.

A policeman was standing nearby and as I stopped to look he waved me on with a gentle movement of one finger. "Nowt for you to see here, lad. Get yerself off to school.

But I could see. People were buried under there; that was why they were digging holes in the rubble, and there was an ambulance waiting with its back doors open. I hurried on.

When I reached the main road it, too, was partially blocked. A bomb had fallen on the convent school tumbling half of it into the highway and slicing open the building where the nuns lived. Holy pictures and crucifixes hung on the walls of upstairs rooms that no longer had floors. Different coloured patches of wallpaper marked the different rooms. I was staring up at what must have been the nuns' bedrooms, private places now brutally ripped open for everyone to see. And what was worse, there were iron bedsteads half sticking out of the rubble. Were the nuns lying buried under there? More men were digging into the piles of debris.

I nervously skirted the rope barriers around the spilled-out bricks and hurried on. From the city walls I looked down on the devastated railway station and the smoke that was still drifting from the ruins. The girders that had once carried the great, Victorian, glass roof over the platforms were just a tangled jumbled mass. I felt a guilty admiration for the German bombers – they had flown all the way from Germany in the dark and blown our railway station to bits.

Not all the German bombers had been so accurate on their bombing runs. Near the river a warehouse was a smouldering shell and the old Guildhall on the opposite bank had lost its roof. I crossed the river, ran along the bank and turned up Marygate to school only to find a blackboard propped up on the pavement.

'To all pupils,' said the chalk message, 'return home and you will be notified when you can come back to school.'

I looked down the passage that led into our playground and discovered that my school had gone; it was just another pile of bricks, broken timber and plaster. Complete shock was overtaken by bewilderment and then delight. Hurrah for Hitler! No more school!

Father had also been sent home for the day, because the railway station had been put out of action. Throughout the city a lot of people had been killed, probably about eighty, said the rumours, including nuns in the convent. There were whispers that the worst casualties had been in a housing estate that straddled the railway line, on the outskirts of the town. There the houses had been victims of the near misses on the station.

Mother's main concern was getting back to normal and buying bread and milk before it all disappeared, but the road to the shops was still blocked by an unexploded bomb. The ARP wardens had been round and told everyone that the bomb was inside a house just two streets away, and that it could go off at any time.

We turned on the radio and found we were on the BBC news.

"Last night German bombers raided the ancient city of York. There was a number of casualties, but only minor damage was caused."

I was aghast. How could they say that? The BBC was telling lies? And then the announcer added, "The world famous cathedral at York escaped damage."

"What!" cried Father shouting at the wireless. "You stupid idiots! Fancy telling them that! That's what they were after, you twerps! They'll be back now. You see!"

Five minutes later there was a knock on the door. It was an elderly neighbour from the opposite side of the street.

"Have you heard what they said on the news?" The old man was almost beside himself with rage. "Of all the daft things to say."

Other people in the street were appearing at their front doors anxious to share the same views. They were all convinced that the Germans were only interested in bombing cathedrals, and as they had been told that they had missed ours the first time they would be back. We were certain of it. Then three Spitfires roared over our street in formation, but instead of cheers they only provoked mutters of disapproval. "Where were you last night when we needed you?" demanded our neighbour

We were having tea when the unexploded bomb exploded. An ARP patrol car came round with a loudspeaker on the roof telling everyone not to be alarmed; it was not the start of another air raid.

"Good," said Mother. "Now I can get some bread."

I went with her. The street barrier had gone, and when we looked up the street where the bomb had been there was yet another gaping hole in the row of houses, and another horrible pile of bricks and plaster. Only then did it strike home. That was someone's home and all their possessions, all their toys, had just vanished. Where were they going to live? Wales with its mountains and gorse-strewn fields was another world and another life.

We bought some tired looking bread from the shop and that made me feel even worse. Here there were no baking smells to tingle the taste buds. I thought of Uncle Bob, with his spiky eyebrows and his hairy arms slamming pieces of dough into the tins? This sad little loaf that I was carrying did not come from my bake-house. That was far, far away, warm and safe, undisturbed by the long, terrifying whistle of descending bombs.

When we got home with the bread and milk Father was oiling the wheels on the old pram that he kept in the work-shed. For years its only use had been as a kind of wheelbarrow for moving things around whatever garden we happened to have.

Towards dusk he brought it up the yard to the back door. Mother, meanwhile, had been busy in the kitchen and she put packages of sandwiches and vacuum flasks of hot tea into the pram. Father appeared with the family cash box and some papers, and they, too, went into the pram along with gloves and scarves.

I watched and said nothing.

When it was dark Mother said, "Wrap up real warm, because we're going for a walk. And take your flashlight."

And walk we did, taking it in turns to push the pram. And very soon we were out in the country. We stopped in a lane and sat on a fence and waited. It was cold. At one o'clock we ate the sandwiches and drank hot tea, but there was no ominous droning in the sky. At 3.30am Father said, "I don't think they're coming."

So we walked slowly and sheepishly back home and crept back into our darkened street, quietly letting ourselves back into the house.

Eighteen

Our school 'holiday' did not last long. A week later there was a letter saying that I had to report to another school on Monday at 8.30 a.m. precisely.

"That's a girls' school," said Mother in disbelief.

And so it was. As we stood outside our new school, with the teachers checking names, there was not one girl in sight. The headmaster, Mr. Cooper, was still in cap and gown, but his cane was missing. We wondered not too hopefully if it had disappeared under the pile of rubble that had once been our school. We were a quarter of an hour into our first lesson when there was a lot of noise outside. One of the boys parted the net curtains and peeped out the window.

"Girls!" he whispered. "Hundreds of 'em."

That caused such a rustle of interest that the teacher turned and caught the boy at the window, ordering him back to his desk. The headmaster's cunning plan became obvious. The boys arrived at 8.30 a.m. and the girls at 8.45 a.m. and after that a meticulous plan went into operation. Our moral welfare was protected by a miracle of time-tabling, which ensured with frustrating efficiency that we hardly ever saw a girl.

As we boys poured into one end of the gym we would see the doors at the opposite end swinging shut as the last girl departed. Play times, too, were segregated. But there was one memorable moment. We were lined up to go back indoors after one play break when a girl, a real live girl, came into full view in the play ground. She must have been late for a class and was taking a short cut, only to be confronted by the boys *en masse* and on parade. Instantly there were howls and whistles. The girl panicked, slipped and fell and there was a fleeting glimpse of black stockings. Whistles and wolf howls pursued her as she fled.

The wrath of God - and what turned out to be far worse - the wrath of the headmaster fell upon us. For a whole week our break times were cut short as a punishment for 'disgraceful, ungentlemanly behaviour.'

The war went on, but the Germans paid us no more visits. Regularly the sirens would sound, but 'they' were always 'passing over.' We listened to that distinctive droning in the sky and with first hand knowledge pitied those on the receiving end.

As the months went by the tenor of those nightly tones changed. The flat countryside around the city sprouted airfields full of bombers, ours, and the noises in the night sky grew louder. Four-engined Halifax and Lancaster bombers massed above the city nearly every night and headed out to bomb Germany. Their noise was different, a steady roar rather than the pulsating drone of the Germans.

It was common gossip that the RAF bombers used the cathedral as a marking point for the outward journey. I did fleetingly wonder sometimes what sort of hell all those planes were creating for the Germans, but so what! They had bombed us.

One night in the city centre Mother, Father and I came out of the cinema and bumped into a crowd of airmen noisily spilling out of a public house. They were drunk and started playing leapfrog in the roadway and generally sky-larking about. I had never seen grown men laughing, shouting and behaving like that. Mother was disgusted, but not Father. "Don't begrudge them a bit of fun. It might be the last they get. They could be flying over Germany tomorrow night."

I stared at the raucous gang noisily acting the fool. These were the heroes we read about in the newspapers and they were not very old; but for their uniforms they looked like the older boys in our school when they were larking about in the play ground. And tomorrow night they could be over Germany in the dark, being shot at and chased by enemy fighters. Tomorrow night they could all be dead.

Father had a new job inspecting signal boxes and making sure the equipment was in order and that the signalmen knew their 'rules and regs.' This had an unexpected bonus; everyone wanted to keep well in with the visiting inspector. Real eggs were back on the menu instead of the dried ones that came in packets. The signalmen nearly all kept hens and sometimes pigs, and that meant not only eggs, but sometimes a bit of bacon. This was an unheard of luxury, and I was told that I must never ever boast that I had had a real, fresh egg, otherwise Dad and everyone else could get into the most dreadful trouble. So an egg, carefully boiled for six minutes and sitting there in its egg cup, was a rare and treasured thing, all the more so for having to be eaten in secret.

Mr. Waite, the fruit and vegetable man, supplemented our diet by coming round once a week with his horse and cart and supplying potatoes, carrots and turnips. He brought other gifts, and by our back door was an old bucket and shovel just in case the horse 'obliged.' The pile of steaming manure had to be collected in the bucket for our tiny back garden. There was keen competition, for these droppings were in great demand.

A 'fair shares for all' arrangement developed, but one with a competitive edge. If the offering was deposited right outside your house it was yours, but in the middle of the road it went to the first shovel to arrive on the scene. As a result the horse's slow progress down the street would be watched from front room windows; everyone was 'Digging for Victory' and all gardens needed fertiliser.

Mother, watching at the window would give me a quick call and chase me out of the house with the shovel and bucket. But the old lady across the street usually beat me to it. I was a gentle soul, and seeing her puffing across the road at a lolloping run with her apron flying always made me feel guilty.

"You've let her get it again!" Mother would complain. "Honestly! Why can't you be a bit quicker?"

The old lady across the street usually beat me to it.

The peace and calm of Wales was fading from my memory. I had never seen a soldier in Wales, here they were everywhere. And there was also the disturbing sight of my middle-aged Father dressing up in his badly fitting army uniform. He had joined the Home Guard and had to take it in turns to man the anti-aircraft rocket guns on the race-course. One night when he was on duty we, and most of the city, were awakened by a dreadful screeching sound followed by two sharp explosions up in the sky. The gun battery, with my Dad on duty, had opened fire on the enemy. I felt very proud that he was out there defending us, even though, curiously, there had been no sirens and no droning approach of enemy bombers.

I waited eagerly over breakfast for his return. When he did appear he was in a bad temper. It had been his gun that had gone off – in error - and he had been put on a charge. I was horrified. Was my father going to jail?

"I did everything by the book, but the damn thing just went off," he protested. "Bang! Flames everywhere and two rockets - gone! And the Sergeant said it was my fault."

Later in the day an army despatch rider parked his motorbike outside our house, slowly took off his leather gloves and extracted an official envelope from his pannier. This, I thought, was the summons for my father's court martial. It was, instead, a letter from his Commanding Officer, a well known elderly, local solicitor who was also the town's coroner. The gun had a faulty safety circuit, he said, and that had caused it to go off prematurely. The charges were being dropped. Mother thought it was very kind of the colonel to write personally. Father did not take up her suggestion of sending him a thank-you letter.

The months and the war were ticking by. Letters kept arriving from Wales, and Mother would read them out to me with her glasses on the end of her nose; Aunt Nell or Aunt Kate would always send their love. Uncle Bob was still working all by himself in the bake-house and I wished nostalgically that I was there with him.

Father and I had discovered a way of getting a close-up glimpse of the war in action. We got out our bicycles as soon as it was dusk and rode out to the airfield, a few miles out of town. The public road ran alongside the runway, and in the half darkness we saw the bombers waiting at their dispersal points, their engines growling gently: big, black, exciting silhouettes in the gloom. One by one they slowly made their way from their pads and circled the perimeter track until they reached the end of the runway. There they paused, as if hesitant about what they had to do next. I used to wonder what the pilot was thinking as he sat up there in the cockpit waiting for the signal. And then the engine noise rose to a frantic shriek and the black shape hurtled away into the darkness, clinging for a long time to the safety of the ground before tentatively, reluctantly lifting into the air. We sat on our bicycles and watched them for ages.

"Let's hope they all come back safely," said Dad. "Poor devils."

Not all of them did. One morning when it was still dark we were awakened by the rumble of a distant explosion. One of the returning bombers had missed the runway in the morning mist and crashed onto a farm house, killing the occupants. Rumours were whispered about the horror of it. Burning fuel had rained over the fields setting cows and sheep alight; they had scattered in flames burnt alive as they ran. And it had all happened not far from where we used to watch.

One night when the bombers were going out at dusk, and the whole sky was trembling with their engines, there was a huge explosion and the whole house shook and rattled. Mother and I disappeared under the staircase, landing on top of each other in the rush with all the brooms and brushes falling round us. There was no siren and when there were no more explosions I went out into the back garden. Black smoke was rising a short distance away. I could see all the aircraft droning overhead and they were ours. There was no doubt about it, by now I was an expert on aircraft recognition.

I got on my bike to see what I could find out, pedalling as fast as I could towards the column of smoke. The ARP wardens had not yet had time to put up barriers so I got closer than I should have done. First, there was a light scattering of mud and bits of wood on the road and then bricks. As I cycled around a corner there it was - a crater that looked like the opening of a volcano. Two houses had vanished into a deep smoking hole. This could be no ordinary bomb.

I stood and stared dumbfounded, people were beginning to arrive including a policeman on his bicycle. "Where do you live?" he demanded in quite a gentle tone for a member of the constabulary.

I pointed back the way I had come and his mood changed.

"Then get yourself back home again double quick. Off with you!"

We learned later that it was one of our own bombers laden with fuel and bombs that had fallen out of the sky. Five people in the houses died and all the bomber crew.

There was a knock on our door one evening. A very tall, shy Canadian soldier was standing on our doorstep. He was one of Father's Scottish cousins two or three generations removed. His Mother had emigrated years ago and married a Swedish farmer in Saskatchewan. The union had been blessed with the birth of a son, our visitor, and somehow he had obtained our address from his Scottish relatives.

Mother made a great fuss of him, and he called once a fortnight and had supper with us. Despite rationing Mother always managed to produce something. Usually it was a 'fry-up' - an English version of Welsh 'stunch' - a mixture of mashed potatoes, bits of vegetables and corn beef all pressed flat into a big frying pan and cooked on both sides until almost black. Sometimes our visitor would bring bottles of beer.

He was a Presbyterian, a strict teetotaller, and because of this he had become a steward in the officers' mess. He always dashed off at 10 p.m. to catch the last army lorry waiting in town to take the soldiers back to camp.

Then he told us he was being moved down south; we never saw or heard from him again. I often wondered if he survived the war.

The country was building up for D-Day. Everyone knew it was coming and the signs were everywhere. We were miles from any possible embarkation port, but half the dual carriageway just south of the town had become a huge vehicle park. We used to go and stare at them in wonder - hundreds of lorries parked side by side stretching nearly ten miles towards the next town.

There were no guards, but then why should there be? No-one would have dreamed of touching them; they were for our soldiers; they were for the war. There must be lorries, tanks and guns parked like this all the way south to the invasion ports, we thought. It was an awesome sight. God help the Germans when this lot was unleashed.

Father told us he was going to be away for a week on something secret and not to tell anyone. Off he went with a small, battered suit-case containing his pyjamas and shaving things, leaving Mother and me alone and bewildered. What was it about? He was too old to be in the real army. He was very circumspect about it when he did return and I only learned about it later.

The Guards Armoured Division and their tanks had been practising for D-Day in Yorkshire, and then had to be moved south for the invasion. Father's job was to make sure their tanks were loaded safely onto flat railway wagons.

He had been very impressed with the Guards. "The officers get off the train first, then the Sergeants. The Sergeant Major yells, 'Guards – de-train!' and all the soldiers get out together and line up on the platform in columns. Bloody marvellous to watch!"

The next time he disappeared 'on war work' he was with the Americans who were also moving their tanks around the country by rail, preparing for the big day. And this time he came back with goodies – chocolate and candy bars with cartoon characters on the wrappings. And then something amazing. He unwrapped it carefully. It was a sandwich made with white bread. The last time I had seen white bread had been at Uncle Bob's. Since then we had only eaten the grey, gritty wholemeal National Loaf, which the Radio Doctor assured everyone did not cause boils.

This sandwich was a startling, almost dazzling white. Someone had taken a bite out of it, leaving a clear impression of their teeth marks, but this did not dampen our amazement. It was preserved in our house for ages as a symbol of American decadence.

Nineteen

I left school and it was assumed that I would be joining the railway, and I would train to be a civil engineer. The interview was very odd - a crowded office full of big desks and telephones, and busy men in dark suits. My interviewer was on the telephone and beckoned me to sit down beside him. As the phone conversation went on he grabbed a piece of paper and scribbled on it a simple fraction sum followed by a question mark. He pushed it across the desk and indicated that I should work it out. I did so easily. While still talking on the phone he wrote down more questions and so the interview continued.

Had all my years of education come down to this? When he did put down the phone he checked all my answers and read a letter from my headmaster. "Bill Scott's lad, aren't you?"

"Yes, sir."

The telephone rang again and he was immediately in conversation elsewhere. This did not stop him rummaging in his desk and producing what I saw was my application form to join the great and famous London and North Eastern Railway. He wrote something on the form and handed it to me while putting his hand over the telephone mouthpiece, "Doctor's - room 206. Give him this."

I had passed my interview and written exam. I went to see the doctor. He tested my chest, looked in my ears and told me to cough, and then he put out all the lights and asked me what colours were flashing at me from a device at the other end of the room. I had no idea and made a few vague guesses. The lights came on again and the doctor was looking a bit embarrassed. "Sorry, lad. You've failed. You're colour blind."

Colour blind? What did he mean colour blind? My application form was stamped and returned to me. Clutching it like a death warrant I made my way to my Dad's office. As soon as I went in he saw the look on my face.

"I can't see colours, I've been failed."

Father took the application from me and read it. "It's OK. I've just got to tell someone - be straight back."

And he was. "Not the end of the world. Nobody was to know. We'll sort something out."

My career on the railways had hit the buffers before it had even got up steam. Mother refused to believe it. She produced threads of different coloured wool and demanded that I named them; she was going to show that doctor. Then anger and disbelief turned to incredulity. Where she saw green I saw brown or was it fawn? Certain colours were clear, but not others. I suppose the railway doctor feared I would drive a locomotive straight through a red light or connect the blue wire to the green and cause mayhem. I wondered miserably if I were destined to be a baker after all. At least I could tell the difference between white and brown flour.

In the gloom that followed Father read that the local newspaper wanted a copy boy; 'with prospects of becoming a reporter,' said the advertisement. Mum, slowly recovering from shock, said I had always been good at 'composition' and that I should give it a try.

My headmaster reluctantly wrote another letter on my behalf whilst asking with a sniff, "Whose idea was this? Why don't you get yourself a nice steady job at a bank?"

He had clearly forgotten the day when he had torn up my mental arithmetic paper.

And so I became a trainee journalist, which sounded a lot better than 'copy boy.' The interviewing technique at the Press was even more perfunctory than the LNER's, and I soon realised why: there was a trial period of three months during which I had to show 'aptitude'.

The Press was in the town's main street: a three-storey, half timbered, medieval structure, with the linotype and printing presses buried deep down in the basement. For some reason the subeditors' room was as far away as possible, at the very top of the building.

On my first day I climbed flights of worn stairs to this room and as I entered faces looked up at me. Some very serious-looking, old men, most of them wearing woolly cardigans, were sitting around a huge long table, which was littered with papers. A little man at the head of the table beckoned me forward; he had a waistcoat on under his open cardigan. "That's your place there." He pointed to a small table with three chairs around it. "The others will be here in a minute, or they'd better be!" And he looked at the clock.

I sat down and studied the men around the subs' table. These were the people who sorted out all the stories that went into the paper, and they looked seriously clever and self-assured. I wondered if any of them were colour blind. They were all reading bits of paper and marking them in pencil.

Then I saw a dog under the table, a very large red setter. That accounted for the strange smell I had noticed when I came in. The dog saw me looking at him and it started banging its tail noisily on the ground. Its owner without even looking down or stopping work pushed the dog with his foot and the tail wagging stopped. The silence was oppressive.

"Rubbish!" one of the men shouted, screwing up a bit of paper and throwing it at one of the biggest wastepaper bins I had ever seen, propped up in a corner He missed and the ball of paper joined several others lying around the bin.

Two boys arrived, Peter and Derek, only to be ticked off by the chief sub for being late. "Show John the ropes and next time get here on time."

Peter talked posh and gave the impression that he was only passing through, and destined for greater things. His condescending attitude annoyed me. If he were so posh what was he doing here? Derek in contrast seemed subdued and not very happy.

"Copy!" said the subeditor with the dog, dropping a wedge of paper into the wire basket in front of him. Peter nodded at Derek in a lordly fashion.

"Come with me," Derek said.

I learned that at the cry of 'Copy!' my job was to grab the papers from the out-tray and rush them down to where the men worked on the hot, metal, linotype machines. There they turned these bits of paper into lead 'slugs' for printing.

Derek and I delivered the story to Mr. Armstrong, the man in charge of the linotype operators. "New aren't you? Watch and learn."

He put a mark on each of the half sheets of paper I had brought down from upstairs and gave one sheet to each of about a dozen of the linotype operators. Minutes later the words on paper had been converted into print slugs, which were all gathered up and put on a galley. Mr. Armstrong ran an ink roller over them and handed me a galley proof.

"There you are, lad, that's the first story you've dealt with. Take it back up to their lordships. But first, have a word with George over there on that first machine."

"What's your name and address, mate?" asked George. I told him and his fingers flicked over the keys of his linotype machine. Lead slugs dropped into the tray beside him. "There you are - a souvenir of your first day at work."

They were still warm to the touch. Perhaps it was the memory of another warm smell that made the aroma of hot metal printing so exciting. So was the sight of the giant printing presses, with their huge rolls of paper silently waiting for 'press time.' Derek took me down to the machine room late in the afternoon when press time approached.

The machines were huge; to be near them felt like being in the bowels of a great ship. At the touch of a button the giant stirred itself and the paper slid up and over the rollers, gathering speed until they blurred and the whole building, right up to the subs' room started to tremble; even those detached from it all in the front office felt the tremor. At the far end of the great throbbing machine the newspapers came out on a moving belt to be snatched and sorted ready for despatch. Every day it happened and it created an aura of excitement and achievement, as if something new and wonderful had just been born.

For my part in this creative process I perfected a technique for transporting copy at speed down to the basement without actually touching a stair. They were all short wooden flights, and by sliding my hands down the banisters as far as I could while keeping my feet on the top step I found I could swing from landing to landing rather like a miniature Tarzan in the jungle. Once when told that a particular piece of copy was needed urgently I took the run at even greater speed than usual. A portly gentleman slowly climbing the stairs had to fling himself back against the wall as I crash landed on his hallway. I shouted, "Sorry," but did not stop. The news had to come first.

When I returned I found the subs' room in a state of amusement. The portly gentleman was the Editor and he had been telling everyone about his near miss with a flying copy-boy. Apparently he thought I was a very keen young man.

The three of us - Peter, Derek and I - were classed as trainees, but we were really just messenger boys taking copy, galley proofs and photographs to every part of the building. Sitting at our little table in the corner of the subs' room we quickly got bored, so we developed our own literary skills. This involved making 'ancient' documents in the form of pirate treasure maps. The secret was to toast them carefully over the electric fire until they became convincingly brown and aged. No-one seemed to mind this activity until one of the 'maps' caught fire. As the floor was always littered with bits of discarded paper we nearly set the whole building alight. It was only then that this formidable group of serious old men in their woolly cardigans realised that we really existed. The one with a smelly red setter under the table said very loudly that somebody should be training us; just because his dog had got his tail singed.

Each of us was adopted by a subeditor; we had to sit beside him watching what he did with the reporters' stories before we dashed downstairs with them. We were learning 'how to sub', but fiddling about with someone else's writing was boring. The really exciting work was done by the people in the next room, the reporters. They were out and about seeing things happen and writing about it, not sitting around a table inserting full stops and commas.

There was a reward for our training endeavours. The paper did two-sentence reviews of all the films in the town's cinemas, and the proprietors provided two press seats for the critics. These free tickets brought something new and exciting into our lives - girls. There were several of them in the front office selling advertisements, more manning the telephone switchboard and some slightly older ones in the copy room typing up the stories being phoned in by reporters. And there were the posh ones upstairs - the secretaries.

On Fridays, when the cinema passes were allocated, we three copy boys went on the prowl with all the evil intent of Greeks bearing gifts.

But the girls were wise to us. "Which one of you has got the Odeon?" naming the best cinema in town.

If all you could offer was a free seat at the local flea pit your romantic hopes were dashed for another week.

Peter flaunted his public school superiority and scorned the inducement of cinema passes, but still managed to cut a swathe through the female staff. His particular fancy was June, the petite and rather plump girl on the telephone switchboard. When the door to the telephone room was left ajar, which seemed to happen quite often, he would stand there watching her slotting the cable plugs meaningfully into the telephone sockets. Softly he would start whistling, *"June is bustin' out all over"* - a tune from an American musical - and she would laugh and eventually push the door shut with her foot. We were full of admiration for his cheek.

We did get to do some longer pieces of writing ourselves. Wedding forms would arrive en masse several days before the actual ceremony. When the real reporters declared themselves too busy with more important things the wedding forms were dumped in our laps; we were told to write them up and make them different. This was easier said than done. How many different ways could you say that X married Y, but various permutations came into use: X married Y at St Cuthbert's Church today ... St Cuthbert's Church was the setting for the marriage of X and Y....

And while still striving to be different: The bride who was given away by her father wore ... Given away by her father the bride wore ... Wearing a dress of ... the bride was given away by her father...

At least it taught us alternative ways of constructing sentences. Always, amongst the pile of repetitive, boring details on the wedding forms we had to be on the lookout for anything unusual. Failure to spot that someone of local importance was getting married or that there was some unusual feature to the event brought humiliating cries of, "Where's your news sense, lad?"

My subeditor soon spotted my disinterest in the subbing trade, and in response to my pleading I was let out into the big, wide world, but only down to the magistrates' court to collect copy from Mr. Foster the court reporter. He was large, slow and grey haired, a former policeman who had exchanged the beat for the press box. I had to tip-toe into the court and slide in beside him as quietly as possible, so as not to interrupt proceedings. If the press box door squeaked there was a fierce glare from the Clerk of the Court, a former colonel turned solicitor, who regarded the court room as his personal world.

Sometimes I had time to sit and listen to the proceedings while Mr. Foster wrote up the cases. He did this as they unfolded, prosecution and defence carefully recorded with a stub of pencil on a neat stack of numbered and catch-lined half sheets of paper. So when the presiding magistrate gave the thief in the dock a stern lecture and fined him £20 all Mr. Foster had to do was record the result on yet another half sheet, marked 'Theft Intro' and add it to the rest of the paperwork. Slowly he would fold all the papers in half and hand the completed story to me with a nod. The next prisoner would come into the dock and Mr. Foster would have his shorthand notebook ready. I marvelled at the unhurried speed of the man.

My shorthand and typing improved at twice-weekly night school classes. I was one shy boy among dozens of girls, all of whom were hoping to become shorthand typists and secretaries. We typed in unison chanting our mantra: left hand a s d f g - right hand semi colon l k j h. There were no letters on our typewriter keys so all our eyes were lifted up to heaven or rather to a huge diagram of the key board pinned high up on the wall at the front of the classroom. The teacher was a lady of powerful physique, dark haired and with heavy black rimmed glasses; I imagined her as the terrifying matriarch of some office typing pool. She patrolled our lines of desks, her approach marked by the increasing aroma of orange perfume.

It was a curious feeling, having been so uncomprehending in company in Wales, suddenly to become so acutely aware of everything now being said around me. It was as if someone had taken the wax out of my ears and it was exciting. I listened and wrote the important items down in my newly acquired shorthand.

Out with a senior reporter on his rounds I listened, and wrote down all the important news in my newly acquired shorthand. I went on morning visits to the police station to hear a recital of the town's overnight crime, and I became an inquiring bystander at just about everything that happened in the town. It was a busy world and I was part of it and it was fun.

But shadows were looming. My eighteenth birthday was approaching and my world was about to change again. D-Day came and went and, as if by magic, the lines of tanks and lorries on the roads outside the town shuffled away south. Then the war in Europe was over and everyone went slightly mad.

There was dancing in the street, but for me it was a strange feeling of mixed emotions. The war was over, but I was about to be called up. My friends and I had narrowly missed being involved in a huge historical event, all the heroes of which were coming home again. And where were we going? We were going into an army with no war to fight. And then one of the subeditors reminded us, "That's one down, lads. Only the Japs to go now."

And that was a shock. We had not given much thought to the Japanese. Surely that was an American affair? The impending approach of my call-up papers struck a frisson of alarm. Surely they would not send me to Japan? Was I destined to face some crazy Japanese soldier fanatically defending his homeland with a bayonet? Amidst all the dancing and jollification of VE Day and the end of the war in Europe that did not seem fair.

We were playing tennis in the park, one Saturday morning, when someone shouted excitedly from the upstairs window of a nearby house, "Hey, lads! The Japs have packed it in. The Yanks have dropped an atomic bomb on 'em."

And we all whooped and cheered like Red Indians. A hundred thousand people - men, women and little children - had vanished from the face of the earth, turned into cinders in one ghastly blinding flash. We did not know the details nor did we care. The war was over, really over, and by the grace of God we had missed it by a whisker.

Twenty

Call up papers were dropping through letter boxes; friends a few months older than I had already packed their battered suitcases and gone. It was a strange feeling - childhood brought abruptly to an end by a brown envelope lying on the front doormat. Selfishly I never considered what my parents might be thinking about their only child leaving home; my mind was filled with the excitement of going off to be a soldier. But when Mum and Dad suggested we should go back to Wales for a family holiday I realised something that was not being put into words. It was probably going to be our last holiday together. Even so I went cheerfully enough, the last rite of childhood; memories stirring of fresh bread, distant mountains and the sea.

We got out of the early morning train at Afon Wen and there was the same cold sea lapping at the edge of the same deserted platform; another chill dawn was breaking over the same bleak pebble beach. I could not believe it, and when the same milk van appeared bumping towards us down the country lane it was like watching the slow re-run of an old film.

We climbed on board the train from Harlech in total silence; even Father was subdued. And when we arrived at the station there was, as before, no-one to take our tickets or carry our bags. We stood outside the railway station with our suitcases while Dad looked in vain for a taxi. Across the road was the shop where my Auntie Mima worked and it was closed like everything else.

In the corner of the station there was a tiny office with the word 'Taxis' etched on the glass, but the door was locked. A piece of paper on the door gave a telephone number, but if there was a telephone on the station it had been cunningly hidden. We walked several hundred yards towards the seafront before we found a kiosk. Mother said we might just as well walk the rest of the way, but Father insisted on ringing the taxi number.

"Get up, get up!" he said down the phone, but the taxi driver snored on. Father left the phone swinging off its hook, still ringing.

"Gordon Bennett, what a place," I heard Father mutter.

Mother went on ahead saying nothing and we walked, carrying our bags, resting every hundred yards. After a sleepless night on the trains Father was getting more and more angry. We came to the seafront where the beach and the dunes had crept even closer since I was here last. Mother was well aware of Father's growing irritation as we approached our gaunt B& B on the front. "I hope we're not too early."

"They'd better be up," said Dad grimly. "I told them what time we were coming and I want my breakfast."

Thankfully the boarding house was awake and the lady who opened the door was friendly. We humped our bags over the threadbare carpets on the stairs. My room was tiny, but it had a view of the sea. Then I heard raised voices downstairs. Father had just discovered that breakfast would not be for another hour. The cook did not come in until eight o'clock, but we could have a pot of tea in the front lounge.

Slowly we unpacked to fill in the time and the eventual arrival of bacon and eggs mellowed Father's mood. Overhearing snatches of conversation I gathered that Father had not wanted to spend a precious week of his holidays in Wales.

It was Mother who had had wanted to come back – 'hiraeth' she called it - a sad Welsh word, which meant a powerful, nostalgic longing for home. And it was then that I made a disturbing discovery: somewhere deep inside me lurked that very same feeling. And that was very worrying. I did not want my emotions to be tied to this place.

"I'm going for a walk." I wandered along the beach and threw stones at the sea and thought deep, sad thoughts.

Aunt Nell was still in her grey, pebble-dashed terrace cottage, but somehow it looked smaller, and so did she – as if she had shrunk into less space. We were all greeted on the doorstep and ushered into the front room. There were the same ornaments on the mantelpiece and the same pictures of Victorian angels on the walls. And there was 'my corner' where I had pinned my maps and attempted to make my Spitfire.

We had tea and drop scones served on a tray and it was all very formal and polite. When I went upstairs to the toilet I peeped into my old bedroom. The bed had gone; it had been turned into a kind of study. It was all very strange. This had once been my home, but I felt no nostalgia for the house, and that made me feel slightly guilty. I felt I had outgrown it.

Throughout the visit there had been some talk in English for Father's benefit, but most of the conversation was in Welsh, as usual, including one animated session accompanied by much eye rolling and gestures of disgust by Aunt Nell.

After tea our walk around the town continued. "What was all that last bit about?" asked Dad. "Something about a new minister was it?"

Father must have been trying to follow the Welsh.

Mother laughed. "The new chap isn't married, but his fiancée keeps visiting and staying overnight. Nell wants the chapel elders to do something about it."

And now Dad laughed, "She's a right one to talk."

Mother gave him a quick look and no more was said.

I was intrigued. What did he mean: Aunt Nell was no-one to talk? Father had some questions to answer when we were alone.

We wandered the shopping streets apparently aimlessly, but drawn along by some invisible force, which was gently pulling us to one inevitable destination. We reached that familiar narrow passage between the houses that led to the bake-house, but to my surprise Mother walked straight past and headed for Auntie Katie's.

I hesitated, but I had to follow.

The shop window with the crumpled net curtains, the suspended pine shelf and the same scattering of bread and crumbs; nothing had changed. The bell above the door vibrated on its spring with just the same noisy sense of alarm. And standing behind the counter like someone frozen forever into one of those sepia-toned Victorian photographs was Aunt Katie. It was as if she had never moved since my last visit. Her mouth dropped open in shock. "Helen bach."

Her fingers went to her lips and I thought she was going to cry. Instead it was words that began to flow. Then I came under her sad, searching gaze. She spoke in English, "All grown up you are now."

To save my blushes the door bell clanged again and a small man in a white apron came in with a full bread basket on his shoulder. My heart gave a little skip of panic. It was not Uncle Bob. Why wasn't it Uncle Bob bringing up the bread? Had something happened to him? The man's quick dark eyes looked at each of us in turn. He recognised Mother immediately and put down the basket, wiped his hand on his apron and held it out for her to shake. "Helen, isn't it?" And off they all went in Welsh.

While he talked he was rapidly taking the bread out of the basket and expertly stacking it on to the shelves. I watched, fascinated, and noted the different types of loaves were all going in their usual places. That at least had not changed.

Ivor, for that was the man's name, turned to Father and myself. "Like to see the bake-house, would you?" Slyly he pointed a finger at me. "Bet you would, eh!" I nodded. "Come on, then."

The empty basket was up on his shoulder in a flash and we were off in single file up the street and down the passage I knew so well. The long, low whitewashed bake-house with its tiny windows set in its thick stone walls was waiting to meet us, passive, unchanged. Ivor heaved the stable door open with his shoulder and we followed him in. There was another man standing in front of the table where the dough was kneaded and this was not my Uncle Bob either.

"This is Ellis," said Ivor. "Very deaf he is. Won't be able to hear you."

Ivor shouted introductions in Welsh and Ellis stopped kneading two pieces of dough and slowly wiped his hands on his apron. Solemnly we shook hands, Ellis at the same time pointing to his ears and shaking his head.

"During the war did it. He's going to get hearing aids. Hearing aids, aren't you?" Ellis repeated in a shout.

Ellis sensed the explanation and grinned at us before giving a double thumbs up and going back to his kneading. Meanwhile I looked around the bake-house with some curiosity.

"You remember all this?" asked Ivor.

I nodded. It was the same - even to the alarm clock in the biscuit tin with its face showing through a hole hacked in the lid. I never knew why it lived in there unless it was an attempt to protect it from flour dust.

"Left school? Working are you?" enquired Ivor.

"I'm a trainee newspaper reporter."

"Not a baker, then?"

"Too hard work," I said. "And you get burned fingers."

Ivor translated this slowly and loudly for Ellis and they both chuckled.

"Where's Uncle Bob?" I asked. "Is he all right?"

Again my words were translated in shouts for Ellis's benefit.

"He's not too bad," said Ivor. "You'll see him for yourself soon enough."

There was a quick exchange of glances between the two men.

"Got on well with him, did you?" said Ivor. "When you were helping him, that is…"

I nodded, and again there was the loud translation into Welsh. I knew the reason for this quiet interrogation - Mother had told me some time ago about the gossip when I had been the baker's assistant. In a town where everyone knew or was related to everyone else the rumour had gone round that the young English cousin - me - was being groomed to take over the bake-house. And that was disgraceful, the gossips said, because I was taking away the jobs of Ivor and Ellis while they were away fighting for king and country. The gossip died a natural death when I disappeared from the scene.

Ivor appeared curious about my days in the bake-house during their absence winning the war. He watched carefully as I showed Dad around pointing out the paddles that were used to bring the scalding hot tins out of the oven and graphically recounting how I had burnt my hands on them. "Uncle Bob had bits of rag to wrap around my fingers," I explained.

Ivor heard me. "Still do that," he called.

"Get yourselves some proper gloves?" said my ever practical Father.

Ivor winked at me. "You tell the boss when you see him. 'Gloves cost money,' is what he says."

The two men were now both kneading dough and slamming the lumps into tins. Throughout the war years Uncle Bob had done all this by himself. Ivor beckoned me over and in dumb show indicated that I should mould some bread myself. I tried and as usual got the dough stuck all over my hands. And that quietly delighted them both.

Mother appeared and there was more hand shaking and chattering in Welsh.

"Come and see us whenever you want," Ivor called to me as we left. "Still find you a job."

My brief excursion into their world, while they were busy elsewhere winning the war, had been accepted and forgiven. The bake-house was thriving and everything looked the same, but somehow it was not. Where was Uncle Bob?

Five tomato soups on a tray.

Twenty one

We got back to the hotel as someone banged the brass gong in the entrance hall: lunch was being served. We were the only three people in the dining room; an elderly lady dressed in black with a white cap came in bearing not three, but five tomato soups on a tray. Three of these were set before us and the remaining two were put on an empty table near the window. And there they remained.

Our next course arrived - a slice of beef drowned in thin gravy, new potatoes and some hard carrots. By the time our sweet arrived the tomato soup on the other table had congealed. The waitress cleared away the two dishes shaking her head and muttering. We learned a useful lesson that day - lunch in this hotel was served at 1 p.m. whether you were there to eat it or not.

We were invited to Butlins! There was a telephone call to our hotel from Aunt Mima to say that day-passes for all three of us would be waiting at the gate and we should bring our bathing costumes. Aunt Mima had left Bon Marche and was now personal secretary to the camp manager. Butlins had taken over an old army camp a few miles along the coast.

When we got off the bus by the front gates we saw huge fences enclosing brightly coloured huts and buildings, and there was a strange looking cable system, running cabins slowly over the sand dunes to the beach. Cartoon characters were perched on the roofs defiantly trying to look cheerful.

At one of the two 'guard houses' we found our passes were indeed waiting for us, and we all entered the camp with amused disdain and a distinct curl of the lip. Father was in mocking mood. "We haf ways of making you laff," he said in his best German accent.

We passed determinedly happy families on bicycles as we skirted a distinctly chilly and uninviting outdoor swimming pool.

In the slickly modern reception room we met Aunt Mima, and very smart and businesslike she looked in her black suit. She was clearly someone of importance at Butlins, judging by the deference shown to her by everyone else. She had not changed from her days at Bon Marche; what fascinated me was the perfection of her make-up. She shook hands with Father, hugged Mother and then surveyed me at arm's length before tapping the side of her cheek.

"Give your decrepit old auntie a kiss right here," she laughed. "You're too big to get all lipsticked like last time. I've got my reputation to think of."

Aunt Mima, I concluded, was a different breed to the rest of them in this town. We had quite a day, swimming in the indoor pool, riding the dodgems and then having lunch in the vast dining hall with the loudspeakers blaring happy music. Aunt joined us in the ballroom for the afternoon tea dance - a big band was up on the stage and, above the dancers' heads, a giant glittering ball slowly revolved casting slivers of light in all directions. Mother and Father went twirling off together around the dance floor.

"Come on," said my aunt. "Dance!" I put my hand gingerly on the side of her waist.

"Good grief, lad," she said. "We're supposed to be dancing together not in different countries."

I was swept into an embarrassingly close embrace, but thanks to the instruction books from our local library and Mother's help I made a passable stab at ballroom dancing with the manager's personal secretary.

"Well done," she said when back at our tea table. "That's your duty dance with your old auntie over and done with."

Actually I didn't think she was that old, in fact I thought she was good fun and I said so to Dad on the bus back into town.

"She escaped that's why," he said. "Went to university, got a job abroad, saw a bit of the world, but then this place dragged her back. It has that effect."

Mother did not say a word.

We slipped into a holiday routine, with my parents being unusually accommodating about what I wanted to do. There was a nostalgic repeating of childhood things, picnics on the beach, sand castles and long walks. Dad and I talked like conspirators about our mountain adventures, and then when Mother was not around I picked my moment to ask, "What did you mean when you said Aunt Nell was one to talk?"

He laughed. "Family secret."

"Tell me."

"Don't you dare let on to your Mother that you know."

"Promise."

"Well then," said Dad and then he hesitated. "No better not. Your mother would kill me. Best let sleeping dogs lie."

"Oh, come on," I pleaded.

"No. It wouldn't be fair. Aunt Nell was good to you and your Mum – taking you both into her home like she did. Besides it was absolutely nothing by today's standards... So who cares? Forget it."

"But Dad..."

"Forget it. Time's long gone."

And nobody ever did tell me.

On the third evening of our holiday Mother gently asked if we could attend the nightly family gathering at Aunt Katie's. I agreed eagerly, hoping at last to see Uncle Bob, but he was not there. The gingham table cloth on which his knife, fork and plate had been carefully laid had gone. Instead there was a bowl of flowers sitting on the highly polished table top, and that morbidly struck a disturbing chord of memory; it reminded me of that shiny coffin covered with flowers filling the passage at the family funeral.

The atmosphere of this place was creeping over me all over again. Katie saw me staring at the table and explained that Uncle Bob had eaten earlier and gone out. "You want to see him, John?" she asked me in a shy sort of whisper.

"Yes I do."

"Then you try the bake-house. That's where he'll be most likely at this time. Goes there a lot he does these days. 'Specially at night."

Aunt Nell, plump and queenly sitting in her usual chair, nodded knowingly. After the family revelations, I now viewed my aunt in a new light, but noticed that she was showing vague disapproval at the mention of Uncle Bob's name.

"Is he working?" I asked. "I thought Ivor and Ellis ..."

"Sort of working," said Aunt Katie quickly. "You go down there and have a chat. He'll like that. Off you go now."

I had never seen Aunt Katie so insistent, so I went leaving the rest of the family unnaturally quiet in the tiny, back parlour.

The bake-house door was unlocked, and all the lights were out leaving the place in semi-darkness. A dusting of flour over the tables and work benches gave everything a faintly ghostly air.

"Hello!" I called. I heard some one moving over by the ovens and a growling voice said something in Welsh. "It's me, John."

I walked further into the bake-house. Uncle Bob was sitting on a stool in the furthest, darkest corner, sucking on an empty pipe. He snatched it out of his mouth. I knew sufficient Welsh to recognise a few swear words. Eventually in English came, "It's you, isn't it?"

He was on his feet, pushing the pipe into his jacket pocket. His suit was just as crumpled, and his bushy eyebrows were even more hedge-like, and somehow he seemed smaller.

"Well now then!" he cried. "It *is* you."

And his hand enveloped mine with the same firmness and softness that I remembered, and a twinkle came into his eye. I noticed with fascination the brass stud still dangling from one of the holes of his collar-less shirt.

"On holiday then?"

"I said I'd come and see you again."

"Course you did. And so you have."

There was something odd about him standing there all by himself in the shadows of the silent bake-house, half real, half ghost. This was the place where every day I had seen him dominant, larger than life, weaving his magic, bringing inanimate things to life, kneading and stirring, filling the air with the glorious smell of freshly baked bread. Now in this dim twilight it felt as if the bake-house had slipped into a deep sleep.

"Are you working?" I said tentatively. "Can I help you with anything?"

"Working?" The question surprised him. "No, not working. Ivor and Ellis - they do the working."

"It was just seeing you down here."

He hesitated and looked a little sheepish. "Gets me away from them up there." He gestured towards the shop with his thumb. "Somewhere to go. Nell still up there, I suppose? Can't avoid her, can you? Every night she's there. Can't stand it. So I tell 'em I have to keep an eye on the ovens."

He winked and I nodded, and he nodded, too.

"So why not come down here, eh?" said Uncle Bob looking round the tables and benches. "Spent my life in here I have - so why not the rest of it? I reckon there's a groove in the pavement between here and that damn shop. There's an epitaph for you, eh? Wore a groove in the pavement, he did."

And his words trailed away. The person I had known, that great big bear of a man once so full of life and mischief, now looked lonely and vulnerable. I was upset and did not know what to say.

"But what you did was important, very important" I whispered "You made wonderful, wonderful bread - people queued up for it every day."

He gave a disparaging grunt and the welcoming glow in his eyes died. He sat back down on the stool and groped in his pocket for his empty pipe, and sucked at it in silence. And before my eyes he appeared to be disappearing back into the shadows.

"Can we go for a walk," I blurted out. He was startled.

"What?"

"A walk. Can we go for a walk? It's a bit gloomy in here."

"Gloomy!"

"Yes. We used to go for walks. Let's see if the bats are still flying. And we can have a look at the boats and the cormorants." I trembled a little inside remembering the temper of the man he once was, but I stood my ground. "We could go round by the harbour."

Uncle Bob thought about this for a few seconds.

"Want a walk, do you?"

I nodded. There was a great deal of thinking before he said, "Better lock up, then."

It was only when we got out into the fading evening sunlight that I got a good look at my Uncle Bob. It was not just that I had grown to be as tall as he, but he seemed to have shrunk within his clothes, and he was unshaven. He was wearing the suit he had worn at the funeral. It had been smart then. He took a torn tweed trilby hat from a shelf and put it on his head before he locked the bake-house door.

I popped into the shop setting the bell ringing merrily and opened the back parlour door. Everyone was in their usual place talking earnestly, but with poor Father the odd one out.

"Uncle Bob and I are going for a walk," I announced.

Somehow that caused a flurry of alarm and Aunt Nell wanted to say something, but took too long to say it.

"Won't be long," I said before she could get the words out of her mouth, and I left them to their gossiping.

Uncle Bob and I walked down the street, past the chapel and headed for the harbour, and I could not help noticing that people were staring at us. We must have made an incongruous pair, Uncle Bob in his old suit and torn hat and me, smartly dressed for my holidays.

"Bora da," people called to us, a little nervously as if they were not certain what the reply would be. Some of them stopped as if in surprise.

"Nice to see you out and about again, Mr. Ellis," said one old gentleman politely in English.

A woman spoke to me, again in English, "I remember you. Come visiting, have you? Do him good. Mr. Ellis needs to get out more, he does."

This was said with a stern look in Uncle Bob's direction. We wended our way through these casual encounters until we reached the harbour, where we sat on a bench and watched the cormorants diving for fish. There were long silences between us that made me feel awkward. He had never been like this before. There had always been a constant flow of talk from him, usually about people he insisted were related to me. And always the relationship had to be established before the story could begin. And always I was confused by lists of cousins and half cousins. But now Uncle Bob did not have much to say.

We stared out at the empty harbour.

"Marina," he said abruptly. "Said they were going to build a marina out there. It'll never happen. All talk."

He fell silent. I asked him about the bakery and got some monosyllabic replies, so I told him about my job and how I would soon be going into the army.

"Not the navy, then," he said showing a flicker of interest. "Lot of the family were in the navy. One of your great granddads was an Admiral."

I waited for more details, but none was forthcoming. "Navy," he

155

muttered. "Lots in the navy…" He was silent again. I wondered if he might be thinking about the sailor that Katie never married.

"Perhaps we ought to be going back," I said tentatively. Uncle Bob took his watch out of his waistcoat pocket and consulted it carefully. "Better check the ovens."

We shook hands at the stable door of the bake house.

"You come and see me again, right?"

"Right," I said.

In Katie's back parlour my arrival brought all conversation to an end. Mother was the first to break the silence.

"Was Uncle Bob all right?"

"Yes."

"Talked to you, did he?" asked Aunt Nell.

"Yes," I repeated. Looks were exchanged and comments made in Welsh.

"Is something the matter?" I asked for the atmosphere was thick with mystery.

"He's not been well," said Mother quickly. "Got very run down."

"No, we talked fine."

Nothing more was said until we were on the way back to the seafront hotel and I confessed that I had found Uncle Bob a little strange. "Is he all right?" I asked.

"Not really," said Mother. "He's become a bit of a recluse since he retired."

"What's going to happen to Uncle Bob? He can't spend every night sitting in the bake-house all by himself. It's not fair."

Father grunted, but said nothing.

"Katie can't cope with him for much longer," said Mother. "She'll need looking after herself soon. So we don't know what will happen."

I decided then and there that I had to get away from the emotional clutches of this place. To me everything seemed old, decaying and locked into the past. And the passive, spiritless acceptance of it all distressed me. Uncle Bob had put life and purpose into this sombre world, now he too seemed to be fading into the past; soon he would be another town character only remembered in old photographs and nostalgically recalled during interminable family chats in back parlours; chats that were always about the past, never the future.

My maudlin Welsh blood was now in serious conflict with my father's Scottish ancestry, but I had spent part of my formative youth here. Give me the boy and I'll give you the man, someone once said. Oh please let it not be this! Was I destined to end my days sitting on some Welsh mountain weeping at the sunset, or would the Highland spirit take over?

There was no contest when our taxi took us to the station and we passed the bread shop. Auntie Katie was standing in the doorway waving a handkerchief - a fragile figure dressed in black with her thin, grey hair drawn back in a bun. In the back seat of the taxi I could not keep back the tears.

The train chugged slowly through the mountains and then passed rows of shabby seaside resorts over which caravans were spawning like an uncontrollable growth. But as the mountains disappeared my spirits slowly lifted. This could not go on. It was unnatural. My call-up papers would be waiting for me when I got back home and at that thought my Scottish blood was stirring. To hell with all this gloom and doom.

" Ha' wa' the lads! Fix bayonets and charge!"

But I knew, I knew it was all bravado. It was too late. That place with its mountains and its graveyards! I might shake it out of my immediate consciousness, but I knew it would never go away. Somewhere deep inside me it would always be there gloomily tugging at my soul.

I wondered if it were still possible to join the navy.

Twenty two

Shivering in the morning mist in the soggy grounds of Brancepeth Castle in County Durham, a few weeks later, my thoughts were focussed even more intently on bayonets. There was a row of us, all eighteen year olds, semi-crouched, with a rifle uncomfortably wedged between our knees and our right hands clutching the handle of the bayonet at our belts.

"When I say FIX," yelled the Drill Sergeant, "You do NOT move! When I say BAY you do NOT move! But when I say NETS - you whips 'em out and you whips 'em on."

We tried this several times, trying to get what was little more than a nine inch nail fitted over the muzzle end of our rifles. Our Sergeant, a veteran of the Durham Light Infantry, was scathing about this particular type of bayonet. "In the desert," he told us wide-eyed recruits, "we had real bayonets, great big bastards waving about in the air. Scared the shit out of Jerry, they did." My mother would have fainted at the language.

But even that small, nine inch nail made me nervous. Was I supposed to stick it into someone?

We were lined up for a practice bayonet charge, and despite my earnest desire to be a pacifist there was something chokingly emotional about it. I vividly recalled staying with my other granddad, the one with a cavalry sword hanging above his fire place. In the hall of his house he had a marvellous painting of the Thin Red Line, which showed the survivors of a Highland regiment gallantly lining up, with bayonets fixed, just two deep across the battlefield and marching forward to meet the enemy. It always brought an awe-struck lump to my throat. And here I was now, a soldier myself, lining up with my nine inch nail. But first we had to scream and yell.

"Put the fear of God into the bastards!" shouted the Sergeant. "Yell!"

And he demonstrated with a fearsome shout, "Arrrggg!"

We squealed pathetically like a herd of pigs in an abattoir. German storm troopers would have died laughing. Round the assault course we ran, viciously stabbing sandbags that had done no one any harm. And then we were sent around again with the rifle getting heavier by the minute. A wild, weary lunge and I missed the sandbag altogether and skewered the railway sleeper on which it was hung. My numb fingers shot up the rifle gouging out bits of flesh as it went, leaving the rifle firmly embedded in the wood. Feebly I tried to pull it out, but failed.

The Sergeant was on me in a flash, pushing me to one side, putting his boot against the post and yanking my rifle free. It was thrust back into my hands and I was told to go round again. There was blood splashing everywhere and he had noticed. "That's what I want to see," he yelled at the others. "See that! Bags of blood."

I wondered if it were still possible to join the navy.

There were thirty of us in a long barrack room and we each had an iron bedstead and a metal locker. On the bed were three 'biscuits' - square, hard mattresses - and four blankets, three folded neatly and the fourth wrapped around them to make an oblong-shaped three-layer sandwich. There were no pillows or sheets. All our kit had to be stored in the metal locker and a battered sheet of paper was passed around to show exactly where each item had to be placed. We leapt to obey the order, "Stand by your beds!" as an officer and a Sergeant inspected every locker.

I knew one of my fellow warriors, Ronnie, who went to the same dance hall I frequented back home. He was a body building fanatic and had brought his chest expanders with him. Every night before lights out, he stood by his bed and heaved the springs apart twenty times. The rest of the squad, all stocky miners' sons from the north, watched him open-mouthed. One of them asked me, "Is your mate all right in the head?"

"He's not my mate," I said indignantly.

Ronnie was not with us for long. Despite all his body building exercises he collapsed on the five mile run with badly blistered feet and was withdrawn from the squad and our paths never crossed again. I settled into the good humoured company of a gang of Geordies and Wearsiders, and I learned all the songs of the Durham Light Infantry, roaring them out as we marched, "If it wasn't for the good old DLI boys, where the hell would the army be?"

To which the descant reply was littered with profanities.

My vocabulary was expanding by the day, and with all the drilling, marching, and the infectious pride created by those songs it was astonishing to see how quickly the camaraderie grew. Very soon we felt that we, too, were part of the 'good old DLI' and, we cockily agreed, 'Where the hell would the army be without us!'

The days passed as we became what were known as six-week-killers. If there had still been a war in progress this would have been our basic training before being flung into the front line. I learned how to fire a rifle and a Bren gun, and how to throw two hand grenades into a pock-marked field. I survived light machine gun training, when one of my fellow soldiers standing at the firing point turned and pointed his jammed machine gun at the rest of us, with the lament, "Sergeant, it's not working."

I arrived home in uniform for my first weekend leave. Mother burst into tears and Dad proudly took pictures of me in the garden. At the local dancehall I and a few other squaddies revelled in the envious glances of those still in civilian clothes. The wrench came on Sunday evening, having to leave my warm bedroom, with its sheets and pillows for the cold train journey north, to return to that echoing barrack room and its row of iron bedsteads and tin cupboards. Mother was appalled that we had no sheets.

"It's the army," I said proudly feeling quite the man, as Dad nodded approval.

"You'll get blanket rash," she fretted. "Goodness knows when those things were properly washed. Make sure you put a towel under your face."

"Oh Mother!"

Gloom descended when I joined the crowd of soldiers on the station, all heading back to Durham after weekend leave, and there was not much conversation in the crowded compartment as the train rattled north in the darkness. All of us had to be in by 23.59 hours - one minute to midnight.

Mother always looked after our rail tickets when we travelled; consequently, I now had an irrational horror of losing mine, and I constantly checked that it was in its proper place in my wallet. As the train pulled into the station I decided it was safer to keep it in my hand.

The squaddies in my compartment were on their feet before the train stopped and the compartment door was flung open with the shout: "Eh up, lads! We're here!"

Everyone spilled out onto the platform.

"It's over there!" someone shouted, spotting the ticket barrier, and a mad scamper ensued. I was pushed, stumbled over a kitbag and went sprawling. A hand grabbed the back of my tunic and hauled me to my feet. "You all right, mate?"

"OK." I dusted myself off, and then realised with heart-stopping shock that my ticket had gone. It had flown out of my hand and disappeared among the scurrying feet. It was somewhere on this dimly lit platform or had it been kicked onto the railway line?

I was the last to approach the ticket barrier and the remaining ticket collector was looking back along the platform towards me. Explain to him what happened, I told myself fiercely, you did have a ticket. It's not your fault. But when I got to the barrier my mouth went dry. Two huge military policemen, those fearsome men with red round their caps and the peaks over their eyes, were standing outside the barrier - waiting.

The ticket collector was a grey-haired little man.

"I had a ticket. It was in my hand," I whispered to him. "I got pushed and I dropped it and everyone walked over it and I don't know where it is."

The red caps were on the other side of the ticket barrier waiting for me to step into their territory before they pounced. The old ticket collector looked at me, his eyes holding mine.

"Honest," I whispered.

He picked up a railway lantern. "Then we'd better go and find it, hadn't we?" he said.

I swallowed hard and followed him along the platform. How could we possibly find the tiny half of a return ticket? He stopped after about twenty yards and asked, "Round about here was it?"

"I think so," I said. "But honestly, it could be anywhere. I'm really sorry."

The beam of his lantern swung too and fro.

"There it is," he bent down and pretended to pick something off the platform. He switched off his lamp and led the way back to the ticket barrier. The station was by now completely empty apart from us and the two policeman.

"Found it," called the ticket collector. "Everything's OK."

I stepped through the barrier and two khaki clad giants closed in. "Where's you pass?"

It was examined in detail.

"Cutting it a bit fine, aren't you," said one of them nodding at the station clock. It was twenty to midnight.

"It's not far," I said, but the two men did not move.

Red Caps had a reputation. I wondered if these two would be nasty enough to keep me there until I really was overdue on my pass.

The ticket collector came to my rescue again, "Have you lot done yet? That was the last train. I'm locking up."

The Red Caps dismissed me with a flick of the thumb and I checked in with minutes to spare. My weekend leave had nearly ended in disaster. Now I had the problem of creeping into a sleeping barrack room and making up my bed without getting a boot thrown at me. But someone had already made up my bed. In the 'good old DLI' I learned, that was what you did for your mates if they were late back from leave.

Thankfully I crawled between the rough blankets and then remembered Mother's advice and got a towel from my locker. I lay there with it around my neck, staring at the wooden ceiling, listening as the air was filled with sighs, grunts and snoring. It was a funny old world; thinking about that ticket collector and my unknown bed-maker it was perhaps not such a bad one after all.

Aunt Nell was ill, and Mother and Father had gone visiting and were full of news. I lay on my barrack room bed reading their letter in detail, whilst trying to ignore the swearing contest that was going on around the next bed. This game could be quite educational and the arguments that arose from it became almost intellectual. The competition consisted of two people going face to face with the jury sitting around in judgement. The first contestant said a swear word twice, and the second had to say and repeat a different swear word within five seconds, and so on alternately until there was hesitation or repetition. It got intriguing after the contestants had run through the usual vocabulary: damn, damn; blast, blast, etc. and then the challenges came thick and fast usually prefaced with the cry, "That's not a swear word!"

Some of the arguments in support were quite imaginative. For instance, if certain fairly obvious parts of the human anatomy, male or female, were acceptable as swear words, why not other parts?

I tried to concentrate on my letter. Auntie Nell had had pneumonia, but was getting better under Mother's care. So they were back in Wales!

Uncle Bob had pulled himself together thanks to some elderly lady who had befriended him. He had done the unheard of thing and bought himself a car, and the pair of them went out on drives together. Mother's tone suggested that she was torn between feeling glad that Bob was taking an interest in life again and mild shock that he had acquired a lady-friend. I smiled to myself, firmly convinced that I knew who the lady-friend was. I could just imagine her dragging Uncle Bob out of the bake-house shadows and putting some fun back into his life. Aunt Nell thought the whole thing was disgusting, wrote Mother.

Ivor and Ellis were still working in the bake-house, and they and Auntie Liz sent their love.

Oh, and there was talk of building a marina in the harbour and giving the town a tourism boost.

'No chance,' I thought I could hear Uncle Bob growling: 'Nothing ever gets done here.'

And Mother continued with a review of some of the shops that had closed and others that were still surviving - just. I put down her letter with a pleasurable glow and felt I had completed a walk round the town and chatted with a few old friends. This was alarming. I thought I had decided to shake that sad melancholy place out of my head.

Twenty three

Not content with turning me into a six-week killer the army taught me how to fire an anti-aircraft gun, in the unlikely event that the Luftwaffe made a comeback. As one of an eight-man crew I hopped around the big gun for eight weeks, and watched in awe as our Sergeant instructor rammed dummy shells into the breach with the muzzle almost vertical. None of us eighteen year old weaklings had the muscle power to do that. Once again we were in awe of the veterans who had survived the war.

Our Sergeant told us, "And remember - always polish your boots. Polished boots saved my life in the war."

It was a puzzling bit of advice and one day, while in expansive mood, he explained, "Jerry had me in a prisoner-of-war camp in Poland, and the Russians overran the place. I always had nice shiny boots so the Ruskies thought I was an officer and I got a ride on a truck. The other poor bastards had to walk back and it was bloody freezing. Lot of the poor sods didn't make it - so always polish your boots!"

Despite the torrent of youngsters pouring into National Service every year the army did on occasions put round pegs in round holes. On my paperwork under the heading 'List Special Skills' I had put shorthand and typing.

This had been on the advice of one of the newly demobbed reporters in the newspaper office. "Safest bet in the army is to be a clerk. Get yourself into some nice company headquarters and with a bit of luck you'll avoid all the shot and shell." Being a bit of a wag and a wit he had to add, "Mind you the order came through once, 'Cooks and clerks will be flung into the battle,' and that was a bit hairy."

We did not believe him. Being short and fat we could not imagine

One nervous eighteen year old soldier

him being flung anywhere, but as he had clearly survived the war I took his advice. And someone, somewhere, read my documents. They decided that as I was useless with a bayonet and not very adept with a 3.7 inch heavy, anti-aircraft gun they would throw me into an office, but not any old army office. They flung me into the War Office in Whitehall.

One nervous eighteen year old soldier in an ill-fitting uniform, trying to look manly and self-confident, stood with all his possessions crammed into a canvas kitbag on the platform at King's Cross. It was crowded with people hurrying urgently towards the ticket barrier. There was a frantic bustle about the place that was disconcerting for a provincial. The engine driver was leaning out of the cab of his huge, dark green, gently hissing, locomotive with the letters LNER proudly blazoned on its side. At least that was familiar. These were the same locomotives that stormed their way through my home town on the way to Scotland. I gave the warm, throbbing, green monster a friendly pat, and called, "Thank you," up to the engine driver, just as my Dad always did. The driver put one finger to his cap in reply.

I had never been to London; this was new and exciting, in an intimidating sort of way. It was here that the great main railway line from Scotland finally, dramatically came to an end in a huge, glass-roofed temple of a railway station. It was totally unlike that other railway track in Wales, which ended with a rusty whimper; this railway line ended with a bang, a climax! London, the capital, waited beyond the buffers at the end of the platform.

The first sight of a tube train was unnerving - a slight breeze of warm air sending paper scurrying down the platform, a distant rattling and this 'thing' rushed out from its dark hole. And once cocooned inside this snake-like creature everyone avoided each other's eyes, everyone was locked in their own world. I was not used to this. On our public transport they at least looked at you, acknowledged your existence, sometimes even spoke.

I emerged from a hole in the ground to find myself suddenly, miraculously in Whitehall, with its huge, famous buildings towering above me and the traffic noisily racing by. This was the centre of England. It was from here that the war had been fought and won.

I consulted my instructions. I was not to enter the War Office by the grand front door in Whitehall, but by a side entrance, which was much less imposing.

"Not another one," said the man in porter's uniform, sitting in a glass cubicle. "Where are you heading for, son?"

"Royal Artillery III," I said producing my movement orders.

"Dump your kit in the corner; I'll get someone to take you up."

In answer to his phone call a middle-aged lady appeared and I followed her along marble floored corridors that had all the gloomy cheerfulness of a Victorian hospital. In a noisy rattling lift we went up three floors, along another corridor and into a large office. Several people looked up from behind their desks, all in civilian clothes. The bald-headed man behind the biggest desk turned out to be a Sergeant major and the man in charge. I shook hands with two men and two more women - all civilians.

"Got digs fixed?" asked the Sergeant Major.

"No, I was just told to report here."

"Typical. You can't kip here that's for certain. I'll get you booked into the hostel, temporary. That's your desk."

I had become a cog in the great Whitehall machine.

My year as a trainee reporter had made me eagerly curious about everything around me, but that curiosity was always tempered with an almost arrogant dose of journalistic scepticism. I was eager to know what this little office did and how. I was disappointed to discover that it was little more than a 'machine' for passing around files and writing letters. When some officer said, "I want the file on so and so," RA3 - as we were known - sprang into action and found the documents for him, wherever they might be lurking. I was amazed that so many people could be engaged in such a trivial activity. All the real work, the thinking and the decision-making, obviously happened elsewhere.

In our office everything pivoted around the lady who had met me downstairs on that first day. She was the Registry Clerk. Everything that came into RA3 went to her to be entered in the 'In' book. And everything that went out of that office went into her other book appropriately marked 'Out.' And that was her job. It would have driven me mad with boredom.

The only fun I had was going on a paper chase when a file was demanded that we did not have. Then all my investigative talents were stimulated. First, I called Central Registry for the file's last known location. They had it registered as being at RA6.

"We haven't got it," said RA6, "Central Registry is a bunch of incompetents. We passed it to RA7 weeks ago. Look it's in the book!"

And I would be despatched to some distant office within the building with a red requisition slip, signed by a colonel no less, demanding that the file be handed over forthwith. How, I wondered, did we win the war?

In my many leisure moments I read some of the files in detail. Some had scrawled comments on them by Field Marshal Montgomery himself. I slowly got a hang of the system. Someone would come up with an idea - like arming tank commanders with a Tommy gun rather than a pistol. A file would be opened with an explanatory memo pinned to the right hand side. On the left were comment sheets. The file was then passed from department to department with various people adding their comments and recommending that other people have their say before the file did a huge circle back to where it started. On this particular topic Monty had scrawled, "Take no action." No doubt the file then finally came peacefully to rest.

I wandered the corridors of power on many occasions with a file under my arm hoping to bump into one of my war-time heroes, but it was not to be. The nearest I got to these powerful, invisible people was when I was told to deliver a file to an Under Secretary in his office on the top floor. Here the panelling on the corridor walls had an extra polish and there were paintings of generals on the walls. The Under Secretary's office door was made of gleaming mahogany, with his name picked out in gold leaf.

"Come," said a voice in answer to my knock. I was astounded. The Under Secretary, a small figure in black jacket and pin stripe trousers, had his feet up on a huge desk and was eating a bunch of grapes like some decadent Caesar. There was a fine carpet on the floor and a vast stone fire-place with an oil painting above; a fire was burning in the grate with a brass coal scuttle holding more fuel and ornate fire irons alongside. It looked like the stage setting for a Victorian melodrama.

The Under Secretary paused in his grape munching as I announced the purpose of my visit. One finger indicated the in-tray on his desk in which the file had to be deposited, and the same finger directed me with a wiggle back out through the door. I had at last seen one of the important decision-makers in this great, Whitehall machine: he wore pin stripe trousers and ate grapes.

After two nights in an army hostel with all my kit in storage they found me digs in Kennington. Ma, as she insisted on being called, had two other soldiers in residence apart from me. She cooked us breakfast and was also paid to give us an evening meal, but I opted to eat out at night; the less time I spent in that cramped boarding house in Kennington the better. Besides there was the whole of London waiting to be explored.

The war had not been over long and the city was full of service personnel and still geared for their entertainment. Ma rarely saw us except at breakfast and late at night. There was the Stage Door Canteen in the former Lyons Corner House with free entertainment from the likes of Frankie Howerd, reducing a hall full of squaddies to helpless laughter. London was shabby and dirty, the bomb sites were still raw, but it was alive, and for a soldier it was the place to be.

But it was moving back to peace-time normality. Lyons Corner House for instance wanted their café back and notices went up that the Stage Door Canteen, our second home, was to close. A mini revolution rumbled among the city's soldier population. Leaflets were distributed and a protest rally and sit-in was organised in the Lyons Corner House that had kept open throughout the war.

I thought it would be harmless fun to join in. We invaded the Corner House, ordered tea - no scones - and at a given signal started shouting, "Save the Stage Door Canteen!"

The genteel Saturday afternoon clientele gathered up their shopping and fled.

Suddenly we protesters had the huge, splendid tea-room to ourselves, apart from whispering groups of elderly waitresses in black dresses with white caps and aprons. "Oh, come on, boys," they pleaded. "We don't want no trouble, do we?"

Sitting there in a near empty tea room with only some waitresses for company our protest became a little pointless. Then all the doors were shut and we were locked in: the management had sent for the police. After a nervous wait, the doors suddenly re-opened and those big men in red caps came in and silently lined up along the wall. Everything went horribly quiet. Surely they were not going to beat us up in front of the waitresses?

The café manager was talking earnestly with the Sergeant in charge. I fervently hoped that he was pleading for peace and goodwill, and hoping that his tables and crockery did not get damaged.

The Sergeant listened, nodded and strode into the middle of café and glared at us. "I want all of you outside - now!" he barked. "And I mean NOW!"

Like good little soldiers we did as we were told. The military uprising in central London was crushed without bloodshed and Lyons Corner House got their café back. The Stage Door Canteen was no more.

My life settled into a pleasurable routine. There were still plenty of service clubs open where we could eat; the Café de Paris had dances and shows every night, and I systematically visited all the capital's museums and art galleries. It seemed strange to walk into these great institutions at will. I was only yards from the National Gallery and at lunch time when it rained I wandered the galleries.

In the British Museum I haunted the Egyptian section and stared in wonder at that desiccated body, thousands of years old, curled up in his stone coffin. Despite all their greatness, the museums looked down-at-heel - desperately trying to recover from the neglect of the war years. I did not mind touring museums on a Sunday, but I tried to draw the line at too much culture on a Saturday.

It was then that I discovered that the theatres often gave away unsold Saturday matinee tickets to servicemen in uniform. The ticket booth opened in Trafalgar Square at midday, but as I did not get out of the War Office until 1 p.m. on Saturdays, by the time I arrived all the tickets for the popular shows that afternoon had gone. As a result I spent many a Saturday afternoon acquiring a taste for opera; only once did I get a ticket for a Whitehall farce and was disappointed. It looked silly and tired, as if the actors were fed up with dropping their trousers. At least the opera singers put some effort into their performances.

But on Saturday nights a different world opened up, bright lights, scurrying people, noisy traffic, and ladies in doorways. "Got a light, dearie," they called from the shadows.

Often we wandered through Soho just for the excitement of being propositioned. The great mystery was how much they charged, but none of us ever plucked up the courage to ask.

And there was the even darker side. Looking in a shop window late one night I was aware that a gentleman in a black coat and homburg hat

174

had stopped beside me. He was more interested in me than the window display. I took off and he followed. Then the footsteps stopped and he had gone. I was not too concerned, because I was in a busy street, but when I looked around there he was on the opposite side of the road, still following me. I was not frightened - I was annoyed. Two police officers were ambling towards me, large, slow, unflustered looking characters. I stopped them. I pointed across the road, "That man has been following me."

The man in the black overcoat and homburg hat saw the pointing finger and started walking quickly away down the street.

We watched him disappear out of sight.

"Doesn't seem to be following you now," said one of the policemen slowly.

It was the only time I felt even vaguely uneasy wandering the streets of London. I often arrived back in the capital from weekend leave to find the tubes had stopped running, so I walked across the city from Kings Cross to Kennington, through strangely empty streets, silent shuttered shops, refusing the offers of the rare prowling taxi. I would tip-toe my way into Ma's house as quietly as I could, only to be greeted over breakfast next morning with the accusation, "I heard you come in last night."

Winter closed in and the newspapers were filled with the country's economic woes. The lights started going out even in London. The nation, we read, was practically bankrupt; a fuel crisis struck and the power stations could not keep running. In the great government buildings along Whitehall the lights went out most afternoons. We were issued with two candles each, to keep us working. I mounted mine on my typewriter, sticking them down with molten wax on top of the rotating ribbon spools. The candles revolved as I typed making shifting shadows across the impressive War Office headed notepaper. But it was depressing. Had a great nation come down to this? Even during the war I doubted if government offices had been so regularly reduced to candlelight.

Then came a gift of sweeties from America. It was humiliating. All the young, National Service staff queued up to walk past rows of tables where all kinds of exotic candy bars and chocolates, in brightly coloured wrappers, were laid out in batches. We could choose a batch and take them away in a brown paper bag; a present from America to their poor English cousins for whom sweets were either still rationed or non-existent. It was a kindly thought, but humbling. We ate them whilst loudly complaining that they were not a patch on proper English sweets; that made us feel better.

In the newspapers, the government announced stringent economy measures and job cuts. The civil servants in our office shivered, and not just because of the lack of heating. The cost of the war was coming home to roost, chilling the euphoria that had greeted the end of the conflict. Everything now took on a darker shade of grey.

I was at the Elephant and Castle surrounded by its nightmare mix of converging traffic on Armistice Day, Sunday morning, when 11 o'clock struck. I did not know what to expect. Slowly everything came to a standstill: the buses, the cars and the taxis stopped on the highway; pedestrians stopped on the pavement; buses switched off their engines. The silence that fell over that frantic traffic junction was eerie and everyone seemed frozen, lost in there own thoughts. I felt I knew what they were thinking: of friends killed in the blitz perhaps, or of sons and husbands who had not come home? Standing there in uniform, wrestling with my own thoughts, I felt a fraud. I had missed the war and, thank God, the war had missed me, but here I was playing at being a soldier whilst they were remembering its horrors.

After what felt to be an age the tableau of the Elephant and Castle started to move again like a broken down old movie jerkily coming back to life.

Twenty four

The expected cuts in Whitehall civil servants were announced: ten per cent of them would have to go. There was despair in our tiny office and that was multiplied throughout the building. Lunch-time union meetings were held; people whispered in groups in the corridors. I felt sorry for them particularly the elderly lady in our office who registered all the mail. Her job was her life. "Where will I get another one at my age?" she asked.

And then in the midst of it all, without any warning I got an official letter myself, on War Office stationery, laid on my desk. I was the one who was going. I was to report to Woolwich Barracks, in uniform with all my kit, at noon the next day. I was bewildered, the office staff were bewildered and Ma, my landlady, was bewildered. I was leaving without proper notice. Would she still be entitled to a month's board and lodgings?

Weighed down with full pack, small pack, belt and gaiters, and with everything else crushed into my kit bag, I was once again a soldier - and a miserable one at that - prized protesting out of my comfortable billet. Why did they not leave me to spend the remaining few months of National Service in Whitehall?

I discovered why later, and it made me feel a little better. By some cunning semantics and sleight of hand the National Servicemen in Whitehall had been classed as 'staff,' so removing them all to their respective depots went a long way to achieving the required ten per cent redundancies. I comforted myself by thinking that my removal probably saved RA3's elderly Registry Clerk's job.

The imposing entrance gates and the high walls of Woolwich Barracks, the headquarters of the Royal Regiment of Artillery, loomed before me as grim and forbidding as a prison. The Sergeant in the guard room was dealing with a steady trickle of kitbag, lugging soldiers like myself. "Name? Rank?"

By now I was a full corporal, or in Royal Artillery terms, a bombardier.

"Pick yourself one of the prefabs over there." He pointed far beyond the huge square. "Anyone will do. There should be one with windows still left in. Draw yourself blankets and biscuits from the stores, and report here eight sharp tomorrow morning. Next!"

I found an empty, prefabricated, barrack hut with only one broken window. Inside were ten iron bedsteads, ten lockers on the walls and one wood-burning stove. This was going to be my home until demob day arrived. I dumped my kit on the bed nearest the stove and went in search of the quartermaster's stores. That night I lay in bed shivering under two blankets, with my great-coat as an eiderdown. A chill breeze moaned through the broken window. There was wood for the stove, but no newspaper or matches to light it.

Next morning I got dressed under the blankets, emerging more or less clothed into the freezing morning air. It was an in-bed dressing skill that I perfected over the coming weeks. The cookhouse was found by following the bodies appearing from other barrack blocks and vaguely drifting in one direction. But, of course, I had no knife, fork, spoon and mug - they had long since vanished in my semi-civilian life. The cookhouse staff grudgingly loaned me a set, but I was told I would have to draw my own from stores. After a meal of beans and half cooked bacon I wondered if the effort was worth it, but I could not starve for the next few weeks.

My first parade outside the guard house of Woolwich Barracks was a miserable affair. There must have been about fifty of us, bitterly cold, milling about aimlessly.

"NCO's fall out," came the order and about a dozen of us stood to one side, waiting. Two Sergeants with clipboards marched up and

178

down, counting out groups for various duties: cookhouse, gardening, road sweeping.

More muttering over clipboards and a few NCO's were despatched to various parts of the barracks for duties to be explained when they arrived. Those of us remaining were checked against a list and dismissed. "Report same time tomorrow!"

I wandered the barracks trying to get my bearings, and at one point decided to take a short cut across the corner of the vast parade square. Instantly I heard a distant voice angrily wailing abuse; it took some seconds to realise that the abuse was being directed at me.

A passing soldier helpfully shouted from the walkway, "Get off the square, bombardier, or they'll have your guts for garters. You're only allowed on there for parades."

I drew my replacement knife, fork, spoon, mug from the quartermaster's stores and was told that as I had carelessly lost the originals the cost would be stopped from my wages. I thought I would try out my new eating irons on lunch in the cookhouse, though the smell was not inviting and the clattering even worse. Stew was ladled onto my plate, and then I approached the mashed potato dispenser. The plate had to be held below the level of the huge serving pan and a ladle with potato attached was then banged violently onto the pan edge catapulting the sticky mass onto your plate to join the stew. At the end of the row of cooks was a man, with an aluminium pot, standing half turned and chattering to his colleagues; over every plate that passed, without even looking, he slopped a flood of dubious looking gravy.

"No thanks," but I was too late.

The gravy man seized my plate with one hand and within seconds my lunch was awash with a brown, greasy flood. I looked at it and decided then and there that if I did not freeze to death in my lonely barrack room I would most certainly starve. Unnoticed in the noisy bustle of the cookhouse I dumped my lunch in the swill bin, washed

179

I was too late.

my dirty plate under the running tap in the sink as requested on the big notice, and left hungry. I did not stay hungry for long. I had completely misjudged the resourcefulness of the British soldier and the entrepreneurial skill of Londoners.

When I explored the world immediately outside the barrack walls it was clear that the needs of those within were well known. There were scores of little cafes, most of them little more than a front counter with a cooking range and a row of white, tile-topped tables. For a hungry soldier here was luxury: two thick slices of corn beef with freshly cooked chips and peas, a mug of hot sweet tea and two slices of buttered bread - and all for 1s.9d.

A feeding routine developed: I had tea and toast for breakfast in the cook-house, starved until evening and then ate out in Woolwich town. I alternated my corn beef diet with sausages and beans, but avoided the hot pork pies over which yet another can of gravy lurked. If a hot pork pie customer nodded his head to the inquiring wave of the can the proprietor rammed the handle end of his knife into the top of the crust and poured a river of gravy into the hole. The river flowed for a suspiciously long time before it overflowed. Nevertheless, I decided I could survive until demob.

Occasionally I had company in my barrack room. Soldiers awaiting postings or demob dumped their kit in my hut, and we exchanged stories and reminiscences. They only stayed for a few days before moving on, no-one ever remaining long enough to form more than a passing acquaintance.

And then my mail caught up with me making me feel not quite so lost and forgotten in this great 'redundant file' of a barracks. Everyone seemed to save their letters, those precious links with their former lives, to read or re-read before lights out. Silent figures lying in the gloom on their beds poring over scraps of paper that put them back, at least in thought, into their own safe worlds again.

In my letters I learned that Mother and Father had been back to Wales, yet again. Ivor and Ellis were expanding sales into the surrounding countryside and doing bread deliveries. Aunt Nell sent her love and so did Katie. Aunt Liz had died and her shoemaker husband had gone to stay with relatives in South Wales. Not another funeral for them to attend, I thought.

There was no mention of Uncle Bob and that made me wonder how the romance was getting on. I went to sleep thinking about it and that was probably why I had a wild dream. Uncle Bob and Irene were getting married and Aunts Nell and Katie were bridesmaids. Uncle Bob had given his brass shirt stud an extra polish and was wearing his baker's apron. Auntie Irene had a flowery frock and a big hat, with daffodils on it. The whole town had turned out for the wedding; the chapel was full and the congregation for some reason was singing funeral hymns at the top of their voices under the watchful glare and the flailing arms of the cross-eyed, billiard hall manager. Subconsciously, I suppose, I wanted something happy to happen in that forsaken world, but in my thoughts even an imaginary wedding had to be tinged with black around the edges.

Boredom was now my enemy, and my saviour was the big red number 52A double deck bus. It transported me back after an hour's journey to the familiar sites of the city that I had got to know so well. I could wander the famous shabby streets again and buy peaches off the barrow boys. I could listen to Big Ben striking and watch the boats on the river. But it was travelling back to Woolwich barracks late at night that was the revelation, sitting upstairs on the front seat and seeing another London going by, streets with scruffy shops, people streaming out of cinemas, girls coming out of dance halls, noisy fall-outs from pubs. From the top of my bus I saw it all - an ever-changing, picture-show of night life in the suburbs.

I had never realised how vast the city was, how varied or, sadly, how drab. I would get back to my broken-windowed, little hut and wonder if the whole world was falling apart.

We junior NCO's were rarely employed, and every day I feared that someone would read my documents and see the words 'shorthand/typist.' If that happened I knew I would be consigned to some company office and become a 'nine to five' clerk for the rest of my army service. My days of wandering free between morning roll-calls would be over.

One morning to my consternation the Duty Sergeant said he had found something special for me to do. I had to report to a company office where I suspected a typewriter would be waiting. I announced myself to the sergeant major in the office.

"Nice little job for you, Bombardier," he said. "March that little lot down to the Education College and hand them over to a Captain Walton. Get 'em signed for and bring the paperwork back here. OK?"

He jerked a thumb towards the window and I saw about thirty men in full marching order standing about outside. This I had not expected. "Where exactly is the Education College, Sergeant Major?"

My question was perfectly reasonable in the circumstances, but the response was explosive and blasphemous. Put politely, he had asked how long I had been there.

"Three weeks, Sergeant Major."

The rest of the staff in the small office looked up and I sensed amusement and then some concern among them.

"I can't take 'em," said one of the Sergeants behind his desk. "No way."

The Sergeant Major looked at me. "Out the main gate, turn right, straight on for about a mile, big wall on the right, big gate, big sign: 'Army Education College'. That's a clue for you. Right? Take 'em to reception, Captain Walton. Right?"

"Right!" I was aware that the rest of the men in the office were listening to these instructions with increased amusement.

"Well off you go," ordered the Sergeant Major.

Despite the two stripes on my arm I had never drilled men in my life, and as I walked outside I saw expectant faces crowded against the office window. Suddenly, I realised that being a full Bombardier in Her Majesty's Royal Regiment of Artillery was more than just a device to give a young soldier a little extra money to cope with the high cost of living in the big city. The stripes were meant to give me authority and command over other soldiers, and that was an appalling thought. On close inspection I saw the waiting troops were all eighteen year olds beginning their corps training. I eyed them and they eyed me. I recalled my days as a member of the 'good old DLI', only this time I was in charge. "Fall in!" I shouted at them, and I was startled at how loud my voice sounded. "Attention!"

Boots snapped into position with a crunch. It was curiously satisfying and empowering. Rows of faces were staring straight ahead, but one or two eyes were squinting in my direction.

"Look to your front!" I was beginning to enjoy this. I moved them into a column of three and gave the order, "Quick march!"

It was like driving an express train from the guard's van - a van, which was now in grave danger of being left behind. The squad marched purposefully away and I had almost to run to catch up. Then there were mutterings in the ranks and heads turning. This would not do. "No talking in the ranks!" I shouted.

"But, Bombardier…" said a voice.

"Quiet!"

I dropped to the rear of my marching column and there was a Major in full uniform standing on the pavement watching us go by. I had of course failed to give him the obligatory, "Eyes right."

Meanwhile the men, my men, were rapidly approaching the main gate, and Woolwich High Street lay beyond seething with morning traffic. "Sorry sir," I said to the officer flinging up a salute as I hurried after them.

"Mark time in front," I yelled.

This was terrifying. My 'train' was at least now stationary, but somehow I had to get this column of men across two streams of buses and cars. Did the two stripes on my arm give me the power to stop the mighty roar of London traffic? Apparently they did. I stood in the roadway both arms raised and the traffic on Woolwich High Street came to a stop; my men marched proudly out. I strode alongside them like a nervous mother hen; buses and cars queued behind us or impatiently squeezed past us. The gates of the Army Education College appeared on the opposite side of the road and there was a welcome gap in the oncoming traffic.

Having glanced behind me a few minutes earlier to make sure that was clear, too, I made a snap judgement and shouted, "Right wheel!" The front ranks turned obediently and there was a frantic squeal of brakes behind me. A bus had appeared from nowhere and was alongside us, the driver's face frozen with a look of horror.

"Left wheel!" I yelled.

Fortunately the human instinct to avoid danger at all cost had not been drilled out of these new recruits. They fled to the safety of the pavement without further instructions. The bus went by, with the driver recovering enough to mouth obscenities at me through his window.

I told myself firmly that one did not make snap judgements when marching men through heavy traffic. They stood badly shaken by the side of the road, looking at me accusingly. I had to redeem myself before they mutinied, took a vote, formed a commune and decided to proceed independently. I strode into the middle of the road and once again held up my arms to stop the traffic. What astonished me was that they stopped again.

The squad wheeled across the road and into the safety of the Army Education College. I brought them to a halt outside the main office.

"Any problems?" asked Captain Walton affably.

I thought I had better confess before exaggerated reports got abroad. "Nearly had an argument with a bus when we came in, sir."

His affability faded. "What were you doing? Should be quite safe with an NCO front and back. Where is the other NCO by the way?"

"There's only me, sir."

"That's not right. I'll put in a report," said the captain briskly.

I was instructed to dismiss the men and send them into the lecture hall. They were standing at ease, but were far from easy: The incident with the bus had clearly shaken them. My approach was greeted with a wary silence. What dangers was this incompetent Bombardier going to subject them to now?

I gave my last order as a non-commissioned officer in her Majesty's army with a huge sense of relief, "Dismiss!"

They gave me some curious looks as they trooped into the lecture hall and I got the distinct impression that in the event of war I would not be their first choice as leader in a bayonet charge. So what, I would be out of the army in a few weeks and it would be goodbye Woolwich, goodbye dingy, old London, and goodbye army.

Travelling north in the train with my kit up on the rack and heading for my own home town to be demobbed was a strange feeling. I walked to the barracks from the station; there were hordes of us filing into the old building on the outskirts of town. It was like a factory, soldiers entering at one end in uniform and leaving as civilians - or what might pass for civilians - at the other. They were incongruous creatures in ill-fitting suits and trilby hats, all fancying themselves as extras in a Humphrey Bogart movie. The important thing was that we had all abandoned khaki - we hoped - forever.

At the last section of the conveyor belt through the shelves and racks of clothes and shoes was a bored Sergeant sitting at a table with a pile of travel warrants in front of him.

"Where do you live?" he asked, flourishing a pen and not even looking up.

"I live here actually," I said, truthful to the last.

He muttered something profane as he looked up. "Look lad, use your head. I want a place name to put on this railway warrant. Now let's start again. Where do you live?"

So for some reason I gave him the name of my second home in Wales. Why on earth did I do that? Now he was looking up at me thinking that I was pulling his leg, but I wasn't.

"How the Hell do you spell that?" he said.

So I was home again in my new suit with a one-way ticket to Wales in my pocket. I was back in my own bedroom with real sheets and pillows, and the same picture of a clipper ship in full sail on the wall. My attic playroom was smaller than I remembered it. Being at home again with my parents was odd. I was not their little boy any more. I had ceased to be part of their family routine.

I felt I should be a part of it again, but I had been a soldier, independent, feeding myself, coming and going as I wanted.

"Where are you going?" Mother asked as I went out. Why should I tell her where I was going or what I did?

It was strange. Going back to work was unsettling, too. I had drifted through the army doing what was necessary: enjoying myself, but really killing time; waiting for demob and for life, real life, to begin again. I was not alone - this was the attitude of nearly all National Servicemen for whom the cry was always, "Roll on demob!" It was a right of passage to be endured, and then talked and boasted about interminably afterwards.

But real life had begun again, and it was disturbing to discover that I was once again a generation behind. I had been just too young for the war and now I was just too young for the return of peace; a whole generation was ahead of me. I was in the shadow of returning heroes.

There were new faces in the office, all returned from the war, and in my absence they had confidently settled back into the working world. They told stories of the D-Day landings and of night flights across hostile Europe, and we listened silently, respectfully, enviously. What could I offer? Typing a few letters in the War Office and nearly wiping out a squad under a number 52A bus? Such adventures did not have the same ring to them, so keep quiet, I told myself, keep your head down, your eyes open, learn and catch up. And all the time I had a strange longing to use that one-way railway warrant to that place, which the Sergeant had such difficulty in spelling, and which I had sworn I did not want to see again.

Then I met Meriel. My social life had progressed beyond brandishing free cinema passes around the typing pool, but was still taking a distant, second place to an interest in tennis. This did not prevent me from becoming a floating male in others' social circles, involving innumerable evening dress dances that were the vogue immediately after the austerity of war. At the more formal functions it was the done thing for groups of people to go in pairs, and for one such event Peter in the office asked me to make up numbers. "She's called Meriel. You'll like her."

I did. She was tall, slim, blonde and very pretty, but also very expensively dressed. Her Father, I learned, was a well-to-do farmer and, more to the point, he would be picking her up to take home immediately after the dance. What she had been told about me, her blind date, I shuddered to think, but she was a marvellous dancer and we had a great time.

During the last waltz we danced a little bit closer and I managed to bump - accidentally - into one or two other dancers, so for a few brief, exciting moments we got even closer. At the end of the evening she took her luxurious, beaver lamb coat from the cloakroom and I escorted her from the ballroom.

Outside a gleaming Rover car was waiting with a stout, grey-haired man behind the wheel. He gave me the curtest of nods and pushed open the car door for his daughter. They drove off, my dance companion looking like Cinderella leaving the ball in her coach. Ah well, that was very nice, but clearly that was that.

It was about a fortnight later that Peter, our self-proclaimed, office expert on girl friends and all associated social matters, inquired, "How are you getting on with Meriel?"

"What do you mean, getting on?"

"You were getting on great at the dance. So how's it been?"

"It hasn't been anything," I said. "I haven't seen her."

"What! You didn't ask her out?" He was genuinely shocked.

"I didn't think she'd be interested. Did you see her Dad's car?"

"Nutter!" cried Peter. "Ring her up."

"What's the point!"

"Ring her up!"

So I did.

"Who?" she said.

It was embarrassing having to explain who I was.

"I wondered if we could go out some time…"

The silence that followed was even more embarrassing.

"You took your time. I must have made a real impression on you."

Twenty five

That army railway warrant was getting scruffier by the month, but was still valid when I used it to pay for half a return ticket to Wales. Despite all my emotions about the place I was going back, but only for a few days. I was now part of 'Meriel's crowd' - a group of her school friends who had stayed together into adulthood. They had organised a week in Llandudno heavily chaperoned by a group of formidable mothers. I was included, but it clashed with a fortnight's holiday that my parents had already tentatively planned in Wales with me in mind. A daring compromise was arranged: Meriel would spend a few days on holiday with me and my parents, and then the pair of us would join the rest of the group in Llandudno.

I sensed that my former home would come as a shock to Meriel and I was even more sure that she would come as a shock to it. I saw the look on her face as we stepped out of the station, the gasworks was still reeking of coal tar and the boats were lying like dead fish in the harbour mud. Very little was said as we walked to the hotel in the High Street - the same place where Uncle Bob and I had had our solitary funeral tea. It, too, had not changed; the paper was still curling from the walls and the receptionist appeared vaguely startled that we had actually arrived. We all unpacked.

"Why don't you take Meriel for a walk," suggested Mother. "Show her round."

I did and watched heads turn in the High Street.

"What are they staring at?" Meriel asked.

"You."

En route for the hotel Meriel had taken in her new environment. Once there, she discarded her high heels and her hat with the perky, single

191

pheasant feather; but even then in her fashionable coat her slim figure stood out. We drifted down the High Street heading for the bread shop as I explained, in probably too much detail, all about my Auntie Katie. But the shop was empty, bereft of bread even though the bell on the spring above the front door clanged just as urgently as ever. The door into the back parlour opened and the tiny, black clad figure of Auntie Katie stood there, her hair now more white than grey.

She stopped short and her mouth fell open in shock. "John bach." And her hands fluttered as she patted my arm.

I bent forward and kissed her on the cheek. "I've brought Meriel to see you." I moved slightly to one side in the narrow corridor. It was as if I had brought a being from another planet into the bread shop.

"Oh," said Aunt Katie and then, "Oh," again.

"Hello" Meriel smiled.

But Katie was still staring, lost for words. "Nice to meet you," she whispered at last. "Friends are you?"

A strange question, but thankfully Mother and Father appeared and broke the silence, drawn as ever to the bread shop as if by some powerful magnet. We crowded inside and this time to my grown-up eyes the back parlour looked even more like a room in a Victorian museum.

Aunt Katie disappeared into the lean-to kitchen and the water pipe on the wall rattled as she filled the kettle to make tea. Already she and Mother were talking Welsh, as of old.

Dad winked at us and made talking gestures with his fingers. "You don't want to get stuck here." he whispered.

Meriel was perched on a kitchen chair in her New Look coat, looking like an actress who had wandered onto the wrong stage set.

"Katie," called Dad. "The kids won't want any tea. They're going exploring round the town. You'll see them again later."

So we escaped.

When we were outside Meriel asked incredulously, "Does she

actually live in there? It's so tiny."

"I'll show you the bake-house." I followed that faint smell of bread down the passage to the white-washed building behind the houses and opened the stable door. Two apron-clad figures looked up. They were still there, Ivor and Ellis, stacking and greasing tins.

"Whey!" shouted Ivor in greeting, cheerily waving an arm. Meriel followed me inside and two sets of eyes widened in approval.

"Girl friends, now is it?" said Ivor. "Who's a lucky boy then? Done all right for yourself there, you have." He wiped his hands on a floury piece of rag and shook hands with Meriel. "You don't want anything to do with that one," he said nodding towards me. "He'll be no good in the house. You'll never make a baker of him, not from what we've heard."

And there were winks all round. I had clearly enlivened their day by bringing them a visitor. Ivor gave Meriel a conducted tour of the premises while Ellis, cut off by his deafness, continued greasing the tins and following the tour with a smile on his face.

"How's Uncle Bob?" I asked. Ellis must have lip-read my question for both the bakers laughed.

"He's got a girl friend, too," said Ivor. "Silly old sod's getting frisky in his old age."

I was about to say that Uncle Bob had had a girl friend for sometime, but something stopped me. Perhaps this was another lady-friend and not the Auntie Irene who had gone with us on our picnic.

"She's done him a power of good," said Ivor. "Used to spend all his time moping around in here at night. Right depressing he was. Right misery."

I hoped it was Irene who had brought about the transformation.

After a while I sensed that the two men wanted to get back to their baking. I made excuses, and said we would come back again. Meriel left the bake-house first, with the two men putting their thumbs up to me behind her back.

We rejoined my parents and walked back with them to the hotel.

"Uncle Bob's got a girlfriend," said Mother.

This was obviously the big news in town.

"We know," Meriel and I chorused.

"Good for him," said Dad. "Who cares what Nell says?"

I was intrigued. What was Nell saying now?

"Nell's worried the woman is after his money. That's what's bothering her," said Dad.

Mother who was always very sensitive to criticism about her Welsh relatives leapt to Nell's defence. "I'm sure she thinks no such thing," she said indignantly. "She doesn't want her brother making a fool of himself, that's all."

So Father held his peace.

Meriel and I were paraded around the family relatives and then Bob suddenly appeared at the hotel as bullish as ever and loudly apologetic. "Didn't know you'd arrived, Helen," he protested.

He sat with us on the uncomfortable settees in the hotel lounge and had tea while we chatted, a twinkle in his eye and quite like his old self. "Got a car now," he announced. "Take you for a ride I can, but only two of you that is …"

"You take Meriel and John," said Dad. "Meriel hasn't seen the countryside round here."

"Right," said Bob, "tomorrow afternoon it is. We'll have a picnic." And he looked at me with a conspiratorial grin.

He breezed out shouting cheerio to the manager behind the reception desk and leaving Father laughing. "Got that, did you? 'I can only take two of you.' That means the lady-friend must be going, too."

The lady friend was indeed going and she was - as I had hoped - my Aunt Irene, looking cheerfully more witch-like than ever in another flowery frock. She came out of her little grey house in response to

194

Uncle Bob's toot on the horn carrying an even larger picnic basket than I remembered. Meriel and I were in the back of Uncle Bob's car and she greeted us effusively from the front seat.

"You're so pretty!" she said to Meriel. "Now has Bob been behaving himself? Not scaring you with his driving, has he? Shows off when he gets passengers."

She turned to the sheepishly grinning driver. "If you don't drive sensibly, Bob Ellis, I'm not coming with you, do you hear me?"

"Get in the car, woman," said Bob winking at us.

As I half expected we drove to the same picnic spot by the river and bumped down the same field to reach the water's edge, accompanied by the same shrieks, laughs and protests.

"John and I will get out the picnic," said Irene firmly. "Meriel you go and watch Bob paddling. He calls it fishing, but it's really just paddling. He likes to have an audience. Makes him feel important."

Bob went off with his fishing rod, and with Meriel in his wake. Irene waited until they were out of ear-shot. "Bet they've been talking to you about me, have they? The family that is. You see I was in Bangor looking after my sister when he retired. I was there months. And he was a right misery when I got back. Missed work, you see, missed the routine. Couldn't leave him moping about like that, could I? For Heaven's sake, what do they think I'm going to do with him?"

"I'm sure they're glad he's happy," I said thrusting thoughts of Aunt Nell out of my mind.

"Course he's happy. And that's what matters, doesn't it?"

The fisher folk returned. "We caught three," said Meriel.

"And threw them back," I said.

"How did you know?"

"He always does."

"Told you! He just comes for the paddle," said Irene.

"Bob!" she called, "Stop pestering those poor fish and come and have something to eat."

They were both wonderful company, happy and chattering, asking questions about my days in the army, my work and then slyly about us.

"Known each other long have you?" asked Irene.

"Not long," I said, and there was an amused silence.

Then it was announced that we were going to Criccieth, a place I had only passed through on the train. But first we stopped at Irene's pebble-dashed, grey terrace cottage to return the picnic basket.

"The toilet's down the garden," Irene whispered helpfully to Meriel, as I waited my turn in the front parlour. Irene's home was like a doll's house - a rag mat on the stone-flagged floor in front of the fireplace, and a mantelpiece filled with silver framed photographs. A table, with a vase of flowers and one place mat set on it, stood in front of the tiny window. And by the fire was a leather easy chair with another small table alongside on which rested a wireless set, a magazine and some unfinished knitting. It was a tiny house for one person. I imagined her sitting there on cold winter nights all by herself knitting and listening to the radio and it gave me a little shiver of sadness; but then I remembered that eventually everything in this place made me feel sad.

But there was no sadness walking down the front at Criccieth eating ice-creams in the sunshine, and with the Welsh flag fluttering bravely from the battlements of the castle. That flag amused me; the castle might once have been Welsh, but it has been captured by the English king Edward I; so, hurrah, the natives had finally got it back again. And that set me wondering: whose side was I on - the Welsh or the English? I then thought of my mother and felt guilty about the answer floating to the top of my mind.

Uncle Bob drove us back to our hotel. Our few days' holiday came to an end and Mother and Father saw us off on the train for the delights of Llandudno. Meriel had passed no serious comments about my temporary Welsh home or my permanent Welsh relatives. She was still strangely silent as the train pulled out of the station and that forlorn harbour that might, one fine day, become a marina faded into the distance. We waited on Afon Wen station, two solitary figures with their suitcases on that desolate beach-side platform. The emptiness of the place closed in around us.

"I just don't understand ..." Meriel began and then stopped.

"Understand what?"

"How people can live here," she blurted out. "It's so depressing. Everything is so grim and run down. And they're so rude."

"They're not rude!" I protested.

"Yes they are. Talking Welsh in front of you when they know you can't understand what they're saying. That's rude."

"That's because they are Welsh," I said. "You wouldn't expect the French not to talk French, because you can't understand them."

"That's not the same thing at all," said Meriel. "Everyone here can speak perfectly good English. And besides, France is a foreign country, this isn't."

"You're wrong there," I said. "They're not English, they're Welsh and this is not England, it's Wales."

"It's still not a foreign country," said Meriel sharply. I took a deep breath. My emotions were in turmoil and I could not understand why. I was feeling hurt and confused; here I was defending a place against which my heart and soul repeatedly rebelled. But it was all right for me to criticise yet I rose to its defence like a stag at bay if someone else dared to do so.

"I know what it is," I said angrily. "They're not posh enough for you, are they? That's what it is?"

By this time in my life I had risen to the status of junior reporter and was rapidly adopting the critical arrogance that all journalists eventually acquire towards everyone and everything. I had also slipped in and out of every level of society in my home town, commiserating with council house tenants driven out of their homes by floods, and sitting in a stately home listening politely to a local Lord complaining loudly about rowdy ramblers on a disputed right of way disturbing his grouse shooting.

I saw very clearly that I lived and worked in a class-ridden society and I had, even then, seen enough of it to understand how sharply contrasting its different layers could be. In contrast Meriel had lived in one world and until now had never seen another.

"Just because they're not rich doesn't mean they're not nice people," I ranted on. "There isn't the money here like in our part of the world. It's not their fault."

There was a long silence on Avon Wen station.

"I think the train's coming," said Meriel.

I married Meriel a year later, but that conversation on Afon Wen Station cast a long shadow and Wales was rarely mentioned between us. Mother listened to the siren song of the distant hills that was always in her heart and when Father retired they went back there to live. I felt sorry for Dad, those buffers in that drab railway station seemed in my morose mind to symbolise a dismal end to a railwayman's working life. I wondered what he would do there to pass the time; if he took up billiards I hoped he would not start whistling again.

The letters kept coming, long cheerful missives, which confirmed that life progressed much as it always had done in the town. And each letter plunged me straight back into that world, stirring up an alarming mixture of acute nostalgia and guilty relief that I had escaped. Meriel watched me reading the letters and wisely said nothing.

Then, whilst we were away on holiday, Aunt Nell died and Auntie Katie slipped away as silently as she had lived. And for me, at that moment, the door of the bread shop clanged shut for ever.

Then there was the problem of what to do with Uncle Bob. Aunt Irene must have died, too, for she was never mentioned in any of the letters, which grew longer and more worried in tone. A great deal of soul-searching was going on. Without Katie to look after him Uncle

Bob had gone into a home and Mother was incensed. "It's pitiful to see him in there," she wrote. "It's not right."

And the next we heard Uncle Bob was living with my parents. "People can talk all they want," said Mother indignantly in her letter. "I'm not having him in there!

Then she added the carefully worded summons, "He's very frail and weak so I don't think he's going to be with us long. I know you loved your Uncle Bob and I thought you might want to come and see him." The unspoken, unwritten, invisible words that followed were, 'before he dies.'

I visited and wished I had not. I wanted to keep my memories of a burly bear of a man sprinkled with flour, crashing tins out of a blazing hot oven. Instead in a big armchair padded around with cushions he was a shrunken version of what he had once been. He grinned and nodded, held out an arthritic hand that was still soft to the touch and talked in whispers. But he tired quickly, his head nodding as he dozed and fell asleep in mid-sentence.

Dad said: "It could be any time."

And a few weeks later that time came.

"I'm going to the funeral," I told Meriel.

"And I'm coming with you. You're not safe to be in that place by yourself at a funeral." Meriel knew me better than I knew myself. I realised that it was not the place that upset her so much as the effect that it had on me; she was always trying to protect her usually rational husband from further bouts of self induced melancholy.'

The town baker was given a big send off and I was one of the pall bearers. I steeled my heart. I was carrying my Uncle Bob; that big man with the bushy eyebrows, the growling voice and flour speckled arms was in this box resting on my shoulder; Ivor and Ellis were along side me. I tried desperately hard not to think. The singing was fervent and the prayers long. Death followed a familiar pattern in this part of the world, but I found I could now let the familiar ritual wash over me. Even the graveyard did not penetrate my defences, nor when I found myself in the same room where Bob and I had shared the sea captain's funeral tea. Ivor was in charge of the funeral arrangements and he sidled up to Mother as the guests gathered, furtively producing a Will from his pocket. "Have a look at that. It's a bombshell."

Mother passed it to Father to try and understand the legal jargon and I read it over his shoulder. Ivor and Ellis had been left the bake-house and the shop, and Mother received everything else. 'Everything else' included a long list of share holdings.

"Could be worth thousands," said Ivor in a whisper. "Where he got it from God knows. Absolute bombshell it is. Nobody else knows about it yet."

"What's it mean?" Mother whispered to Father as people poured in for the sandwiches and cake, everyone talking and the mood lightening as it always did with an interment emotionally out of the way.

"Don't get too excited," said Dad. "The shares are probably worthless. We'll sort it out with the solicitor tomorrow."

But as the solicitor explained the next day, the shares were far from worthless.

"Mr. Ellis was a very careful man," said Mr. Robert Roberts in his office above the dress shop. "He invested only in blue chip shares and only after consulting his bank manager who was a very good judge of the market."

"But where did he get so much money to invest in the first place?" asked Father, totally bewildered that such a huge sum could have appeared from so little.

"Mr. Ellis ran a very successful bakery business for many years," said Mr. Roberts. "And I'm sure you remember his life-style - not exactly extravagant, was he? He spent no money to speak of. His sister ran the shop, as you know, and she drew no wages. It all mounts up and if it is invested well then it grows. My congratulations, Mrs. Scott on your inheritance."

But Mother was far from happy. "When was this Will made?" she demanded.

"During the war," said Mr. Roberts, "Katie was to receive the bulk of the estate and continue to live in the shop, but if she pre-deceased her brother, which she did, then the money goes to you. I can set your mind at rest, Mrs. Scott, this Will was made long before you took Mr. Ellis into your care."

Epilogue

There had to be one more turn of the screw. In their Wills my parents insisted that they were to be buried in Wales, and so it came about, with Father dying first and then Mother. On both occasions standing by their graves in the rain I grimly vowed that I never wanted to return to this place ever again – not even if I came as a handful of dust in a metal pot.

And yet we did go back. We returned tentatively and warily for a holiday. Our young daughter Penny scampered over the sand dunes and helped me throw stones at the sleepy waves. The sun shone and I climbed the Garn again. Perhaps it was the war, I told myself, the war and my maudlin half Welsh breeding.

The town was unchanged, the same boarding houses stood on the sea front, and the same tea-room attracted its elderly gossiping regulars for morning coffee; the fish and chip shop was still in the square, but all the people I had known who had made up this intriguing, heart-wrenching town seemed to have gone.

I decided, then and there, with my young daughter holding my hand, that I had a right to feel nostalgic and maudlin if I wanted to. There was, after all, good Welsh blood coursing through my veins, so being a bit sad and wistful sometimes was in my genes, it was part of my inheritance. I never did learn the language, but I knew the Welsh had their own word for what I was feeling: *hiraeth,* a longing for home. I wandered the town and looked for the last time at the places forever associated in my memories with Uncle Bob and Auntie Katie. I decided that it was high time to leave them all in peace.

Autobiography:

The story of a Swiss girl who becomes a Section Officer in Photography in the WAAF

ISBN 978 1904278 481

Born to a German actress mother and Swiss artist father, Barbara (Bamby) Dallas's life, (née Schmidbauer and Bamberger) was destined to be anything but straightforward.

Part One (1921-41) tells of her rural life in Upper Silesia; and then her school days, after her mother's second marriage to a Merchant Banker of Jewish origin, in a Pestalozzi school in the Reinland and a finishing school in Switzerland. When the Nazis took over the Bank in 1938, her parents fled to England, and Barbara joined them travelling alone via Berlin and Amsterdam just in time for World War Two …

Even though her parents were Enemy Aliens, she joined the WAAF as a photographer, and met her Army pilot husband. **Part Two** (1941-45) is a transcript of Bamby's diary, written whilst serving in the WAAF. She met an Army Pilot during the war and they married just after VE Day. Ian's family insisted he join the family firm of Insurance Brokers, but it enabled them to bring up a family in comfort. In **Part Three** (1945-2005) we see that Barbara's life was never going to be problem or adventure free…

We also learn more about her very young childhood from her stepmother and stepbrother, and the fate of those who did not escape to or stay in England.

EARLY BIRD

by

Richard Mack

ISBN 1904278 66 5

Earlybird is a tongue-in-cheek tale based on the author's fifteen year time as a postman. By turns humourous and disrespectful, the author takes us on a journey into the world of the Royal Mail - introducing us to the eccentricities of its arcane working practices, its employees, its customers and their dogs.

Prior to his employment as a postman, the author was already an *Earlybird*. Throughout this book he brings us delightful yarns of his past life as a market gardener/farmer and other country cameos. And despite the author's scepticism, his enjoyment of his farming years and his time as a postman are evident.

The market town of Bramton could be anywhere in England, and the characters therein could be found in many a rural locality. The story starts one dark, August morning at four a.m. ...

Autobiography:

The story of an RAF Armourer, 1939-1946.

ISBN 1904278329

A Somerset Airman
by Eric Gardner
Red'n'Ritten
for your enjoyment

Eric Gardner grew up in Frome on a small family farm. The *Introduction* to this book is his account of the farm itself, daily routines and the animals with which he shared his childhood, and paints an engaging picture of rural life in 1930's Somerset.

At the age of 19 he joined the RAF. His witty observations of day-to-day life as an Airman in wartime Britain and Canada give a fascinating insight into the life experienced by many ordinary men and women, from all backgrounds, who were brought together by World War Two.

Like many of his generation, Eric Gardner did not receive a higher education, and was unable to fulfil his obvious potential. In later life he often commented that the RAF had been his university.

Eric thought his wartime experiences would be of little interest to anyone else, because he did not see any active service. His family did not agree and encouraged him to commit his memories to paper.

He finished the manuscript for *A Somerset Airman* just days before his sudden death at the age of 82 and so, sadly, Eric never saw it in print.